T...

Hum... alues

by

Cornelius J. van der Poel, C.S.Sp.

PAULIST PRESS

New York / Paramus / Toronto

Published by Paulist Press
Editorial Office: 1865 Broadway, N.Y., N.Y. 10023
Business Office: Paramus, New Jersey 07652

Printed and bound in the
United States of America

Contents

Introduction

In today's world everyone wants to do his "own thing," whether this be to grow long hair and a beard or to have a crew-cut and be smoothly shaven; to wear a mini skirt or a maxi coat; to live in a hippy commune or to be a topless dancer; to participate in a sit-in or to start a hunger strike. These and innumerable other expressions are used to indicate that the individual human being today wants to free himself from rigid formalism and sterile conformity. He wants to highlight a specific aspect or perspective of his own life. He wants to be recognized as a human being in his own right, with a personality which is different from that of others, and with his own value estimation. Many such tendencies in today's society are a reaction of protest against seemingly impersonal, rigid and hollow structures of life which place conventional adaptation to systems above honest feelings and personal development.

This demand for recognition of one's personal development and this search for self-fulfillment are a cause of deep concern for many parents, for civil authorities and for religious leaders. Many traditionally-minded persons consider this movement as sheer rebellion which fills them with confusion, fear and anxiety and which ought to be suppressed. They often try to counteract it, but their counteraction tends to increase the confusion rather than to decrease it. They make every effort to safeguard social and religious values as they have learned and lived them, yet they feel many of these values slipping away from their control.

There seems to be little doubt that the present unrest and insecurity is in the final analysis a search for re-evaluation of the meaning of human life. It would be presumptuous even to try to give a satisfactory answer to the many questions which are raised at the present time. All that can be done at this stage of development is to join in this search.

We do not believe that the past was empty, superficial and useless, but neither do we believe that the principles of the past can simply be used as meaningful guidelines for today's approach to life and religion.

Pope John XXIII opened a window of the Church to let in a gentle breeze that could take away some centuries-old dust. To some it might seem as if a hurricane entered instead, overthrowing and tearing apart all the familiar and sacred. We stress the word *seem*, because underneath the apparent upheaval one sees the current of a deep sincerity. It is the search for the meaning of man in all the dimensions of his human existence. It is the search for man, not merely in his material way of being, but created in the image of God. It is the search for the human task which in and through this human life is meant to be the living and perceptible manifestation of God's inner self.

It is in this search that this book wants to join. It does not intend to provide easy answers, but it hopes to contribute to a deeper understanding of the invitation which God directs to all men. It tries to assist in the search for the human response to this divine invitation which calls men to be the living expression of God's loving presence with humanity, despite human shortcomings and limitations.

We want to use this opportunity to express our sincere thanks to the many students of St. Mary's Seminary, Norwalk, Conn., of the College of Notre Dame of Wilton, and of Fairfield University for their valuable remarks and disagreements during our classes; to the many friends, priests, religious and lay people for their invaluable contributions in private and public discussions on the various subjects; to Father Henry Koren, C.S.Sp., for his painstaking work of correcting and editing; to Sister Rachel Kiefer, F.S.P.A., for the patience and professional skill which she used in typing the manuscript; and to the many others who by their assistance and encouragement made it possible to continue this study of the search for integral human values.

Cornelius J. van der Poel, C.S.Sp.

I
Changing Perspectives in Responsible Human Attitudes

Not so many years ago such customs as "eating no meat on Friday" and "attending Mass on Sundays and holydays" played a very important role in making a judgment about the moral goodness of a person. Anyone who observed "to the letter" the commandments of God and the Church could consider himself morally good. Today the observance of the law "to the letter" no longer impresses people in the same way as it used to do. Today we judge the moral value of a person more on the basis of his involvement in the human community than on his church attendance. The whole perspective of what is right and what is wrong seems to have received a different focus.

The traditional approach to this dilemma of "right–wrong" can perhaps best be summarized in the words of Henry Davis, who wrote in his *Moral and Pastoral Theology*: "Moral Theology is that branch of Theology which states and explains the laws of human conduct in reference to man's supernatural destiny." [1] This description strongly suggests that the human being is a static reality whose ideal perfection can be outlined objectively, and if man wants to be morally good he merely has to adhere to the well-formulated laws which describe his ideal perfection. This approach seems to be based upon a rather strong dichotomy. The relation between God and man seems hardly to go beyond the creator–creature relationship, with barely any room for autonomous human action. God is precisely seen as the supreme legislator who lays down his laws in great detail, and man is responsible for observing them accurately. There is little room left for personal responsibility.

A slightly different approach is taken by Franz Böckle in his *Fundamental Concepts of Moral Theology* where he describes moral theology as "the part of theology that searches for the norms of free human conduct in the light of revelation." [2] If we search for *norms of free human conduct* we leave room for human creativity, spontaneity and inventiveness. The human moral conduct is at least not reduced to a mere observance of laws. However, in the further development and use of his definition the same author makes a sharp distinction between the supernatural goal and source of moral theology and the "purely natural" source and goal of ethics. One wonders whether this sharp distinction does not lead too easily to a polarization in which God and man become competitors. If revelation is seen too much in contrast with "pure nature," then we might come to the conclusion that "revealed" norms of conduct are additions to the "purely natural" norms which man finds in his own being. This standpoint implies that at one time there had been such a thing as a "purely natural human being," to which then a supernatural destiny was added. But there is no trace in history of this purely natural human being.

The book of Genesis seems to point in a different direction. It says: "God created man in the image of himself, in the image of God he created him" (Gen. 1:27). This not only tells us that man has been created by God, but also that man has received a special way of being. Man is different from all other creatures, and Genesis places this difference in man's special relationship to God. No other creature was made in the image of God himself. This means that by his creation man's existence received a special purpose and, consequently, also a special potential. This special potential includes a special task, which is nothing less than to be on earth the created image of God himself.

If we may see God as the creator and as the totally independent source of his own being, then the created image of God himself must have these same qualities in a created way. Therefore, man must have the potential to shape himself in such a manner that the image of God becomes visible on earth in the appearance of man. It took a long period in human history and much divine revelation before man understood the deepest meaning of his own being, but this gradual development and unfolding may not be understood as "additions" to a purely natural human being. If we speak about "supernatural"—or perhaps "transcendent"—and a "purely natural" aspect, we should see them only as two *aspects* of the same *whole* human being. These two aspects are so intertwined that when one aspect suffers, man's "wholeness" is damaged. In this perspective we might describe morality, in the way that Marc Oraison does (quoting Sertillanges) in his book *Morality for Our Time*, as "the science of what man ought to be by reason of what he is." [3] This description takes into account the reality of man as well as his human task and destiny.

Basically the same direction was taken by Vatican Council II in the *Pastoral Constitution on the Church in the Modern World*. Here the existence of man in this world and divine revelation are brought together into one synthesis. The Council describes it as the task of the Church "to scrutinize the signs of the times and to interpret them in the light of the Gospel. Thus, in a language intelligible to each generation, she can respond to the perennial questions which men ask about this present life and about life to come, and about the relationship of the one to the other" (n. 4). The acceptance of divine revelation is a special asset in this search, but it doesn't set the believers apart from the rest of humanity.

On the contrary, revelation leads to a deeper involvement. The Council expresses this by saying: "The people of God believes that it is led by the Lord's Spirit, who fills the earth. Motivated by this faith, it labors to decipher authentic signs of God's presence and purpose in the happenings, needs and desires in which this people has a part along with other men of our age. For faith throws a new light on everything, manifests God's design for man's total vocation, and thus directs the mind to solutions which are fully human" (n. 11).

Revelation and faith, then, are not a superstructure on top of an already existing human nature. Revelation only reveals the depth-dimension of God's presence and purpose which already are contained in the happenings, needs and desires of humanity. The most striking aspect of the Pastoral Constitution is its profound respect for the dignity of the human person. It speaks about "man's total vocation" and about solutions "which are fully human." This is still more succinctly expressed in another section which says: "For God has willed that man remain 'under the control of his own decisions,' so that he can seek his creator spontaneously, and come freely to utter and blissful perfection through loyalty to him" (n. 17). If then we want to search for norms of free human conduct, we can go only to one source, namely, the values of the human person in his total perspective.

Philosophy and Moral Theology

Marc Oraison states that "the ultimate achievement of any philosophy is found in a theory of morality." [4] We may turn this around and say that every approach to or theory of morality is based upon a philosophy of man. Contemporary philosophy objects to looking at man with a preconceived abstract idea of humanity as a basis for the understanding of human qualities. It prefers to look at man in his concreteness in order to come in this way to an understanding of what he is. Philosophical research is concerned with reality—that is, with the totality of all that doesn't exist solely as an object of our consideration. This totality includes not only myself, but also all my surroundings, all human beings, the whole world.[5] Reality stands for everything that doesn't exist merely as an object of the human mind, whether it be visible or invisible, material or spiritual, finite or infinite. This philosophy evaluates also interhuman relationships and what makes man's attitudes responsible or irresponsible. Such philosophical understandings, studied in the light of revelation, should lead us to the perspectives from which we can evaluate what is morally right or wrong from a Christian point of view.

Among the contemporary philosophical systems which try to understand what man is, there are three which are of more importance for our purpose here, namely, existentialism, personalism and humanism. These systems are closely interrelated. We will not try to present a synopsis of these philosophical approaches here, but limit ourselves to indicating from what point of view they contribute to the understanding of the human being in his moral perspective.

Existentialism is concerned with the *actuality of human existence*. It is a way of thinking which is centered on man as an irreplaceable and unique person. Man wants to know who and what he is. He wants to be himself, to think for himself and to express himself in his own personal way. As a unique being, he cannot live by simply following the ideas of others. What "they" think doesn't satisfy him. He doesn't want to "be lived" passively by others, but to actively live his own life. To find what his own life is for him, he starts with the knowledge of his own way of being in his own particular situation. There is here an authentic and honest search which wants to discover what one is in reality, and on the basis of this to proceed to the realization of what one can become in all honesty.

Personalism is primarily concerned with the person—that is, not the abstract concept of the person, but man's corporeal-spiritual existence as the autonomous source and master of its own actions. In its original meaning *persona* meant a "theater-mask" expressing a specific trait or individual. When, under the influence of Stoic philosophy, the idea developed that every individual plays his own role during his life on earth, the word "person" began to be used to indicate the individual human being precisely as having this particular and differentiated approach to life. Being a person includes an autonomy by which man acts in his own right as a rational creature. It also implies the uniqueness which makes this particular human being different from any other. Finally, being a person points to the interhuman relationships in which man recognizes his dependence on his fellow men. This recognition makes him see his life as a "pre-given" reality which, at the same time, is a task to give a responsible expression to his life. It is the purposeful realization of his potential.

Humanism is closely related to personalism, but its main focus lies in the particular place which man has in the existing world. It tries to evaluate man's own position positively. Man recognizes his dependence on other forms of reality, and specifically his dependence on the community of fellow men. The development of the individual human being necessarily demands contact with other human beings. This contact must be *intersubjective* so that it respects the human values of others. Only in the interchange of giving and receiving can full human dignity be achieved. The individual incorporates the human values, but at the same time these values transcend him as this individual being.

These developments in man's self-understanding obviously exercised a strong influence upon man's viewing his responsibilities. The rather strong dichotomy between "body" and "soul" which formerly prevailed has been replaced by a more unified view of the human reality. The insight that the human task has not been outlined in advance, but that it must be discovered by each person together with his fellow men has opened a new perspective on the meaning of law. The understanding that human self-realization and human whole-ness can be achieved only in human interaction has also thrown new light on man's relationship to God. To "please God" no longer refers merely to observing particular commandments, but rather to the totality of man's self-expression. Man's life project now becomes the realization of human values which present themselves in all the ramifications of his life in the human community.

These changes have deeply influenced the study of responsible moral conduct. Moral theology has largely lost its place as an independent theological discipline. Doctrinal understanding of God must be integrated into the norms of human behavior. The Scriptures cannot any longer be approached as sources where we can find commandments, but in the Scriptures we must search for the revealed understanding of human life and of man's task.

This rethinking of moral theology is only in its initial stages, but nonetheless certain general tendencies are manifesting themselves. These tendencies do not contribute different approaches to morality, but are different aspects highlighting a specific angle of the one general approach. We mention here the most important of these aspects to indicate the direction we intend to follow in the following chapters.

Major Tendencies in the Approach to Responsible Human Attitudes

1. There is a search for a unified pattern of Christian life, in counteraction to the multiplicity of commandments. The

multitude of regulations which prescribe human behavior in detail are seen as a fragmentation of human life. They are experienced as impositions from the outside and they easily reduce morality to an external performance. Christ indicates only one basic attitude: "You must love the Lord your God with all your heart, with all your soul, and with all your mind. . . . You must love your neighbor as yourself" (Mt. 22:37–39). The whole law, all the commandments, the whole human performance, are contained in this. This is how Christ interpreted the message of Genesis that "God created man in the image of himself."

Thus Christian life doesn't consist in cultivating individual virtues. So-called virtues fuse into a single reality. Man recognizes God as his creator by an authentic acceptance in faith, while at the same time he realizes that his life on earth does not allow the fullness of self-expression which he desires, but he is confident that he will attain this fullness. To attain it demands that he lovingly dedicate himself to the task that life concretely opens up to him. This loving dedication, which is man's active concern for himself and his fellow men, is the unifying factor which gives meaning to all the rest. We like to call this "love." Perhaps this is what St. Thomas Aquinas meant when he said that love is the "form" of all virtues. Love is that quality which ensures that every good human action becomes a true expression of God's presence with man.

2. This unified pattern of Christian life demands an openness to the whole of human reality. It does away with the narrow concentration upon individual commandments. Instead it looks at the total human vocation. Moral virtues have a character of totality. Every moral action is also biological, economic, artistic, sexual, religious, etc. But these partial characteristics don't constitute any moral value. The true moral value of these characteristics depends on the degree to which they contribute to the concrete expression of the human value in its totality. This view leads us away from a

morality of isolated sins, which always asks "What must I do?", toward an open morality whose deepest concern is, "What must I be?"

3. This concern for unity introduces a third aspect. It is not the individual and isolated action which determines the morality of a person. Just as the individual action must be seen in the total corporeal-spiritual reality of the person, so must this same action be considered in the integral picture of the person's total attitude. For instance, although we need not condone pre-marital relations, it seems obvious that there is a great moral difference between the actions of a couple engaged to be married who are carried away by care and love for each other, and the actions of those who seek primarily self-gratification. In the moral appreciation of the persons as well as of the individual actions, the predominant tone and tendency of the persons may never be overlooked. We may call this the "fundamental option" or the direction existing in the total orientation of life of a person. The primary concern is not whether a person lost "the state of sanctifying grace" in a specific action, but how well he gave expression to his full human dignity. The state of grace cannot be switched off and on like an electric light.

4. What this fundamental option, the predominant orientation of a person's life-expression, means can never be accurately described in objective terms. The individual must rely on the personal judgment of his own conscience, but his conscience must, of course, be correctly formed. The fundamental option goes far beyond the explicit text of laws or regulations and involves the totality of one's personal self-realization. Only in a broad vision encompassing all the ramifications of his life can man gain an understanding of the moral value of his own approach to life. In this perspective will he be able to evaluate his individual actions.

5. The whole life of every individual human being is a continuous search for the "law of being human." If we under-

stand the "law of being human," then in every action the "horizontal" and "vertical" dimensions (if we may call them so) fuse into a unity. In every human action the horizontal interhuman relationship is intended to grow and to develop. In this horizontal growth and development the vertical dimension of God's presence with humanity becomes more clearly expressed. Or, looked at from the opposite side, the effort of man, the image of God, to make God's self-manifestation on earth concretely visible gives depth and meaning to interhuman relationships.

The most striking aspect of these general tendencies existing in the Christian approach to life is their dynamism. Human life can only be human when it is vibrant and active and moving freely. Christ came to fulfill his mission "that men may have life and have it to the full." No straitjacketing legislation or rigid institutionalization should attempt to keep the movement of the Spirit under human control. But neither may the individual claim the direction of the Spirit for himself alone in disregard of the dignity of others and the well-being of the human community. This means that man must search for the meaning of his life and that he is subject to certain norms. This search for meaning and norms will occupy us in the following pages.

NOTES

1. Henry Davis, *Moral and Pastoral Theology*, Vol. I (Sheed and Ward, London, New York, 1958), p. 1.
2. Franz Böckle, *Fundamental Concepts of Moral Theology* (Paulist Press, New York, 1968), p. 1.
3. Marc Oraison, *Morality for Our Time* (Doubleday, New York, 1968), p. 22.
4. *Ibid.*, p. 21.
5. E. J. van Croonenburg, *Gateway to Reality* (Duquesne University Press, 1963), p. 5.

II
Do We Need God To Live
a Good Human Life?

One's first reaction to this title may be one of surprise that the question is asked at all, or at least that it is asked in this form, since many Christians are so convinced that only an atheist will deny man's need of God if he wishes to live as a good man. But the matter is not so evident. For example, let's think of someone whom we know fairly well as a devout man—a Christian. We know him as a person who faithfully observes the ten commandments and the particular commandments of the Church. He never harms anybody, he doesn't steal, he doesn't even gossip more than one can reasonably expect from someone in his situation. But when it is a matter of looking for someone upon whom we can rely for help and to whom we could go in our difficulties, then he would be at the bottom of our list. He doesn't have the human warmth and openness to make one feel at ease, nor any readiness to go out of his way to help others. Yet he is a devout church-goer who observes all the commandments.

We can also think of another person whom we know reasonably well. This particular friend is an avowed humanistic atheist. He categorically denies that there is such a thing as God. When man dies, he says, that's the end of him, and he doesn't expect a reward in an unknown "hereafter." But he feels that during the time he has here in this world he will be fully human only if he does what he can for the betterment of human society. He doesn't pray and never mentions the ten commandments, but in his relationships with others he displays a warmth and understanding, an openness and helpfulness, which make him the confidant of all who know him. In short, he really respects and loves his fellow men as human beings.

The contrast between these two personalities may make us realize that belief in God and the strict observance of divine commandments is no guarantee for living a really good human life. On the other hand, the denial of God's existence doesn't mean that such people are less good as human beings. Obviously, one can find wonderful people among believers in God, and one can find very evil people among atheists. However, the fact remains that the acceptance of God is no guarantee for being good, while the rejection of God doesn't guarantee being evil. Hence, we may seriously ask whether we do need God in order to live a good human life.

We may draw the comparison further and apply it to the material aspect of human existence. Many who believe in God don't suffer more than average hardship, pain and poverty, but their belief in God is certainly no escape from such human conditions. Perhaps even the opposite is true. Those who reject God are subject to the same human discomforts and pains as the believers. In many instances they display the same courage and endurance and patience as those who believe. The answer that the believer will be rewarded in eternal life while the unbeliever will not simply doesn't make sense in this context. From what we see happening in this world we can only conclude that belief in God is no guarantee for moral goodness or material happiness, while the rejection of God is no guarantee of an immoral life or of material unhappiness. Therefore, the question still stands: Do we need God to live a good human life?

If we want to find an answer, we must first consider the meaning of the two terms "God" and "human life." Only thereafter can we try to see whether God is indeed needed in human existence.

I

THE MEANING OF GOD IN HUMAN UNDERSTANDING

It is beyond the scope of this work to try to prove the existence of God. We may hold that a certain form of acceptance of God's existence is a general human experience. Ignace Lepp in his book *Atheism in Our Time* points out that atheists are not unaware of the universality of religious belief.[1] A little further in the same book he states that he has not yet seen anything that could qualify as a positive and constructive atheism. The works that are written to justify atheism are principally, if not exclusively, a critique of religion and belief.[2] Where the unbeliever rejects the existence of God, he still replaces him by some other concept which transcends his own individual way of being, whether it be the good of humanity or the cosmic totality or some other general expression. The individual man in his isolated existence is never seen as the ultimate fulfillment of his being. Therefore, without trying to give any proof we start here with the general acceptance of God. But then the question is, "How should we conceive God?"

This question has always fascinated man. In ancient and primitive cultures the nature and the qualities of God (or gods) were expressed in various mythologies. The description is strongly anthropomorphic, and in many instances the gods are subject to the same hazards as the human beings and ultimately they are dependent on Fate. But whatever form the belief in God takes, it always contains the recognition that man is dependent on powers beyond his control. He doesn't know where the gods come from, nor can he explain their precise way of being. More recent efforts to explain myths in Freudian terminology as projections of the human unconscious don't eliminate the value of religious belief. Even if we say that man wants to be a great lover and therefore projects his wish into a god-of-love, or wishes to be a great warrior and so creates the god-of-war, it still shows a human effort to visualize the invisible and to explain the inexplicable. If perhaps human unconscious needs enter into man's understanding of the nature and the power of God, he still gives witness to his awareness of the essential dependence of human existence on a power beyond his control.

If we can accept that ancient mythology is not just fantasy running wild, but an effort to describe a human experience which escapes physical perception and understanding, then we can see two interesting and important points which remain valid today. First of all, in the myths God is perceived in terms of idealized human qualities. For example, the god of war uses all the weaponry used by man, but God's weapons are much more perfect and his skill immeasurably surpasses human skill. This means that the human desire for perfection and infiniteness together with the experience of his own limitations made man accept that there exists a God who has all the powers which are lacking in man himself. Second, the myths also reveal something about himself to man. They reveal to men what God expects from them. They outline to a certain extent the pattern according to which men must conduct their lives. So it would seem that the same human experience leads both to the acceptance of God's existence and to a certain understanding of the nature of God and his demands upon men.

Both these aspects are still valid today, as Bruce Vawter points out in his article "The God of the Bible." [3] There he says that the God of theology is what we make of him. This was as true in the theology of Chalcedon or Augsburg or Vatican II as in the mythologies of Canaan or Mesopotamia or Phrygia, which fashioned very satisfactory gods for themselves out of an experience of life which some men found adequate and real. This idea is not at all novel. In the Middle Ages Thomas Aquinas (*S.T.* I, 13, 1) pointed out that in this life we know God only through his creation and can describe him only insofar as we know him. This means that we can understand and describe God only in contemporary human terms; otherwise he does not make sense to us. Today, more than at any earlier period in history, we know that man and human knowledge about man are subject to development. If we don't want to call it progress, at least we have to call it change. When human experience changes, man's understanding of God and his approach to God must also change.

Vatican Council II recognized this fact very clearly when it said in the *Pastoral Constitution on the Church in the Modern World*: "Profound and rapid changes are spreading by degrees around the whole world. Triggered by the intelligence and creative energies of man, these changes recoil upon him, upon his decisions and desires, both individual and collective, and upon his manner of thinking and acting with respect to things and to people. Hence we can already speak of a true cultural and social transformation, one which has repercussions on man's religious life as well" (n. 4). These "repercussions on man's religious life" do not merely refer to a difference in the observation of commandments. It is the difference in "thinking and acting"—that is, the difference in human self-perception which is the source and the measure of these repercussions on man's religious life.

In our search for the meaning of God for mankind we must certainly turn to present-day philosophies and theologies. However, it would be a mistake to forget all about the past. Today's way of thinking may be very different from earlier ways of thinking, but it didn't develop independently from the earlier ways. Hence, although today's concept of God may be very different from earlier concepts, it didn't develop independently of them. We may even maintain that there is a progressive development so that the present approach cannot be fully understood unless one has also a general idea of the past approaches.

Developmental Stages of Man's Concept of God

In a very broad outline we may distinguish in human history three different ways of understanding the concept and the importance of God. For the sake of easy reference we shall call them (1) magical understanding, (2) religious understanding, and (3) dynamic understanding. Though these different approaches are more or less linked to specific stages of cultural development, we shouldn't see them as strict and well-defined periods in human history. As Franco Crespi points out in "The Process of Secularization: From Desacralization to Religion" (*IDO-C* 68–9), these three approaches are very much intertwined. When *one* specific approach seems to be predominant, we can always find some trace of the other two.

1. *The Magical Understanding.* This may be considered as the most primitive understanding of the concept of God. God is materialized and localized. The swollen river which sweeps away everything in its path is driven by the power of God—the river contains God—the God of the river. This God is to be respected. He may even demand sacrifices in order to be appeased. Some years ago when I was a missionary in Africa I traveled occasionally along a steep mountain path which was partly blocked by a rare specimen of a hollow tree. In tribal custom and law no one was allowed to pass this "dangerous" spot without picking up some leaves and sacrificing them into the gaping mouth of the tree. Negligence would mean that some accident would occur before the trav-

eler reached his destination. Similarly the meaning of the
fetish is sufficiently known. The fetish is not merely a re-
minder of God's protection, but the divine power has entered into it. It creates, as it were, an invisible protective shield
around the bearer, safeguarding him from attacks by a certain
evil.

Outside this localization (river, tree, fetish) God doesn't
have much meaning. He is totally immersed in and identifi-
able with a specific object or action. God is totally immanent,
and little thought is given to the transcendence of God. This
view largely harmonizes with the concrete way of thinking of
the people involved. It is an approach that hasn't yet completely disappeared from mankind. Although we may never
come across it in this strict sense, we might recognize some
remaining traces of it in the manner in which some poorly
educated people look upon rosaries, medals, etc. We don't
say this to downgrade or ridicule these practices but only to
indicate how a sincere and honest reverence for God is intimately connected with the individual's manner of thinking
and acting. However, such practices can become an obstacle
for the faith in God if they are imposed upon others as essential expressions for religious life. They may easily impress
then as deifications of objects. Then there is a danger that, together with such objects, people will also reject the concept
of God.

2. *The Religious Understanding.* This develops logically
from magical understanding. With *religious* understanding
we don't want to imply that magical understanding is irreli-
gious. We only want to indicate the sharp separation between
God and creation which is prevalent in this approach. It may
be seen as the swing of the pendulum into the opposite direction. Where magical understanding stresses the absolute immanence of God and the identification between God and
object, religious understanding radically rejects this absolute

immanence and identification. God is completely above the created world. He is so absolutely different from the created world that every comparison is sacrilegious. He is the creator of heaven and earth, and everything that exists is the work of his hands. Everything that happens is controlled by him and runs its course as set by him. For this purpose he has put powers into nature, but occasionally he personally intervenes to show his mighty hand, either to punish or to reward. His presence in this world is primarily understood in terms of his being the creator and the ruler. There certainly is an element of love in his presence, but this is mostly understood in the sense that he is the generous benefactor, the rewarder of those who fulfill his laws.

In this religious understanding God's transcendence is absolute and his immanence is reduced to a minimum. There is a certain reluctance to recognize his presence in creation, except insofar as he is its maker. In this religious understanding one is willing to recognize the power and the majesty of this maker in the creatures, but not his inner being. To make a comparison, if we enjoy a good book we'd accept that the author exists and that he is a rather intelligent man. But we'd refuse to accept that this same author reveals in his book his own inner self, his way of thinking and being. The book then becomes a completely objectified production totally separated from the author.

This is what happens in the religious understanding of God. God is considered as the unapproachable and unchangeable. Man, too, is seen as a static reality. His task is to know and to observe the laws which God has placed in nature. Natural disasters and "miraculous" happenings are effects of God's immediate intervention. Storms and floods and epidemics are direct punishments by God, while health, success and riches are his blessing.

This in a few words is the predominant tone of the religious understanding of God. Elements of magical understanding and of a dynamic approach enter into it, but they are placed in an overall picture of absolute and exclusive transcendence.

3. *The Dynamic Understanding.* The dynamic understanding refuses to identify God with any material object, nor can it see creation merely as a product of God's creative power or as a tool in God's hands. It doesn't attempt to deny that God is the creator of the universe, but it doesn't like to say that God *did* create man and things. It prefers to say that he *is creating.* The human reality is not static. In many aspects man is a product of evolution and his actions come forth from an inner source. Man is not bound to any existing form of cosmic reality, but he can produce new forms which hitherto didn't exist, and which didn't result from mere chance. Man is the master of the universe. Within certain limits he determines the course of history and he subjects nature to the progress of human development.

When man's outlook on the world changes, his outlook on God must change also. If world and nature are a value in their own right and governed by their own particular laws, and if man has such mastership over the world, then God cannot be confined to a physical object, nor is the universe merely a tool in his hands. Man's task is more than simply obeying the laws of nature; hence his submission to God differs from simply observing a detailed code of laws. As a result, man's relationship to God and God's relationship to man appear in a different perspective.

Progress in science and technology doesn't mean an elimination of the concept of God from man's life. The more science develops, the more man understands that progress is only possible when he takes the laws of nature into account. The slightest miscalculation in the course toward the moon may send the capsule into the endlessness of space. It is precisely in the progress of science that man discovers his own boundaries, although these boundaries seem to retreat ever more. It is by the proper use of his limitations that man expands his possibilities. Then he can see that the source of it all is not man himself or the contingent physical reality. Then again, the acceptance of God as the source of all that exists is no luxury.

The existing cosmos with all the powers it contains is not merely the product of God's hands but the self-manifestation of his being. The existing universe, including man, is the continuous self-manifestation of the creator who expresses himself in it but is never circumscribed by it. His being is in everything but is not limited by any of them. Perhaps by way of comparison we could say that the mind of the engineer manifests itself in the engine which he produced. In a way he is totally present in every part as well as in the whole combination, but he is not circumscribed by a part or by the whole. This comparison has severe limitations, but it may help us to understand that God's presence in the world is a dynamic presence. It is a continuous communication of existence which makes God totally immanent and totally transcendent. It makes the universe, including man, totally dependent but also autonomous, i.e., existing according to its own laws, having a purpose in itself and acting on a source of inner strength.

The purpose of the universe is not fixed and described in detail from outside, but the world's purpose is outlined by its own possibilities. It must be discovered and actualized by its own activity and evolutional progress. In this light creation reveals not only God's existence but also God's action and God's being. At the same time this dynamic understanding reveals in evolutional development what the human being is and what his task is in this world. This is the view that prevails among theologians today.

Development of the Concept of God in Revelation

"At various times in the past and in different ways, God spoke to our ancestors through the prophets; but in our own time, the last days, he has spoken to us through his Son" (Heb. 1:1). With these words St. Paul tells us rather clearly that God's self-revelation (or communication of knowledge about his presence with men) took the form of a developmental process. We may see this process as the conveyance of God's message in a way adapted to the capacity of the listeners and attuned to the needs of the people concerned. Through insight into the conditions of their time they had to learn about the nature of God and his demands, about the meaning of their own life and about their responsibilities. The richest source of God's self-revelation is undoubtedly the Old and New Testaments. The Scriptures are not primarily written as sources for historical fact-finding, but rather to convey a message to humanity.

1. *The Old Testament.* The first part of Genesis and various other parts of the Old Testament form an anthology of Hebrew literature dealing with the Hebrew understanding of God's relationship to man and man's response to God. The first eleven chapters of Genesis do not attempt to describe actual historical facts, but rather how the Hebrews at that time understood the answers to such problems as the origin of man and the explanation of the present condition of man. Seen in this light, these chapters have a very important historical meaning. They give a true history of thought and understanding about God and man.

If we compare these chapters with non-Hebrew mythology of the same era which tried to answer the same questions, we see striking differences. Where non-Hebrew mythology pictures its gods moved by all sorts of passions and ultimately subject to the blind powers of Fate, the God of the Hebrews appears as the free and totally independent master and creator of everything. He made man in his own image and likeness— that is, man was the special form of God's self-expression in creation. The purpose of man's existence was expressed in his

own way of being. The human way of being included many
limitations, but within these limitations he was personally responsible for the fulfillment of his own purpose in life. The
creation narratives contain a demythologization of man's
ancient beliefs about God.

In the covenant of God with Noah (Gen. 8:22) we see
another aspect of God and the God-man relationship. Although in Noah's story God certainly appears as the avenger
of evil, he is above all the master of the universe, its protector
and preserver, who again conveys his demands to humanity.
In the covenant God made with Abraham we enter into the
era of history about which more facts are known. However,
the historical facts are not the important aspect of this story,
but the message which is given, namely, that God promised
to make him a great nation, even to make him "the father of
a multitude of nations" (Gen. 17:3). God, however, made
his conditions: "Bear yourself blameless in my presence," and
Abraham and his descendants had to bear the sign of "belonging to God" in their body. In the establishment of the covenant with God, Abraham acted with all due respect and reverence, as an independent partner vis-à-vis God. Abraham appears as an independent, personally responsible person who in
his own cultural and national development must be a constant witness of God's presence with men. We see here a
further demythologization of God and a recognition of the
autonomous value of human existence and culture. Human
existence was seen as a gratuitous gift of God, but man himself was the responsible master of it.

In the covenant with Moses (Gen. 19—20) God reveals
another aspect of his own relationship with mankind. The
Hebrew people was chosen to be in a very special sense the
sign of God's dealings with humanity: "You of all the nations
shall be my very own, for all the earth is mine" (Ex. 19:5).
They will be a consecrated nation in which there is an intimate
and sanctifying relationship between them and God. The con-

dition is that they fulfill God's law, which contains the acceptance of God. They must express this acceptance of God in communal activity and in their interhuman relationships. The covenant with God is the freedom of slavery of men, but this freedom implies a personally responsible submission to God which finds expression in their relationship to their fellow men.

Thus the Old Testament progressively unfolds how human life was understood as the special sign of God's presence in the universe. But the revelation of the depth of God's presence was still to come in Christ.

2. *The New Testament.* The self-revelation of God in Christ was the most important step in the God-man relationship. It was a new happening in the history of mankind. But the newness of the event was not primarily that something which did not exist before came into existence, but rather that the deepest meaning of created (and especially human) reality was revealed. This is what St. Matthew points out when he says that Jesus spoke in parables in order "to expound things hidden since the foundation of the world" (Mt. 13:35). What Jesus was and preached had been given to humanity at its very origin, but mankind had never been able to understand it. The longing for God's personal self-revelation was in the deepest and most hidden desires of earlier men who had a deep insight into the relationship between God and human life. Jesus himself told his followers: "Many prophets and kings wanted to see what you see, and never saw it; to hear what you hear and never heard it" (Lk. 10:24).

Before the coming of Christ the believing people were intensely aware of the loving concern of God for humanity in general and for his own people in particular. They knew how he expressed his concern through the leaders of their nation: "You guided your people like a flock by the hands of Moses and Aaron" (Ps. 77:20). Almost the whole Old Testament is one continuous story of sin and contrition on the part of the people, and of punishment and reward, love, mercy and protection on the part of God. He presents himself as the God of majesty and power, of happiness and freedom. But even the deepest religious minds didn't dare to go beyond this influence of love toward man which came, as it were, from outside. The intimate personal presence of God in humanity was beyond their dreams.

This deepest meaning of the human reality was only revealed in the incarnation, as St. Paul says: "I became the servant of the Church when God made me responsible for delivering God's message to you, the message which was a mystery hidden for generations and centuries and has now been revealed to his saints. . . . The mystery is Christ among you" (Col. 1:25–27). The things that had gone before were only pale reflections of what was to come: "The reality is Christ" (Col. 2:17). Of Christ himself it is said that "his state was divine, yet he did not cling to his equality with God . . . and became as men are; and being as all men are" (Phil. 2:6). St. Paul saw Christ as God who lived his divine life in human fashion. Christ, "being as all men are," was fully human, but in his humanity he was the manifestation of God. In Christ God showed his human countenance.

Christ considered his life as a mission which had only one purpose: "I have come so that they may have life and have it to the full" (Jn. 10:10). As signs of the authenticity of his mission he told the followers of John the Baptist: "Go and tell John what you hear and see: the blind see again and the lame walk, lepers are cleansed and the deaf hear, and the dead are raised to life and the Good News is proclaimed to the poor, and happy the man who does not lose faith in me" (Mt. 11:5). In Christ's own words we can recognize the truth of his mission, which is the appearance of God in human reality, by his human concern for those who were in need and by his message about the meaning of life as this was proclaimed to those who did not rely on material riches. It was, however, necessary to have faith, that is, the acceptance of an unseen reality which constitutes the fullness of human life. In a still more direct manner, Christ brought this same idea across to his listeners when he spoke about the final judgment of all humanity. The basis for the judgment is: "I was hungry and you gave me food; I was thirsty and you gave me drink; I was a stranger and you made me welcome; naked and you clothed me, sick and you visited me, in prison and you came to see me. . . ." And further: "I was hungry and you never gave me food; I was thirsty and you never gave me anything to drink; I was a stranger and you never made me welcome, naked and you never clothed me, sick and in prison and you never visited me" (Mt. 25:35–45). In this passage Christ lets God speak, but the norm of judgment is again the interhuman relationship. It is as if God says: If your life on earth was the expression of goodness, care and compassion with your fellow men, you will be in all eternity the created expression of my own being. But if your life was the opposite of goodness, care and compassion, you will be for all eternity the living rejection of what I am. Unselfish human goodness and concern is the measure for the ultimate success or failure of human life.

Christ in Human Life

St. Paul (Col. 2:17) calls Christ the fullness of the God-man relationship which was initiated in earlier stages of human history. Christ, whose condition was divine but who became a man like us, saw that his mission was to bring the fullness of life to mankind. He lived this fullness of life himself in his continuous expression of human goodness and concern for others. Being the Son of God, he revealed to us the human face of God. He didn't bring this personal self-manifestation of God as a novelty, but as a revelation of what had been hidden from the foundation of the world. In the person of Christ, the deeper value and meaning of human reality itself was revealed. Christ didn't assume an abstract human nature, but he was a man of flesh and blood as all men are. The self-manifestation of God in creation, especially in human existence, is made visible in Christ in the everyday life of the individual human being in his relationship to his fellow men and in all other dimensions of human existence. In Christ and because of Christ, daily human life becomes the self-manifestation of God. This is the message and the reality of the incarnation.

The importance of Christ for human life does not lie in the question whether Christ developed a system of ethical imperatives. As a matter of fact he did not. Nor does his importance lie in a theoretical system of doctrine. It lies in the fact that he communicated to us his understanding and the reality of the meaning of human life. From the origin of mankind the human reality was the "image and likeness of God." This means that man was God's self-expression in visible created form. From the beginning, man was to be his own master within the compass of his own way of being, and to carry a personal responsibility for his own way of expressing the meaning of human life. His existence had an autonomous value, but was at the same time totally a gift of the creator. To give expression to this autonomy within total dependency was the task of man.

Man didn't at once fathom the depth of its own significance. It was only in God's self-communication to humanity in Christ that the real meaning and depth of human life disclosed itself fully. Since then man's life in its plain human setting can be understood and lived to its full extent as a participation in the life of God. Human existence in all its ramifications, however material they may be, has become the revelation of God's human life. Human life in its concrete reality and in its concrete human setting becomes "God's living presence on earth" whenever it is lived as the actual expression of God's self-manifestation. Man in his free autonomous activity isn't a competitor of God. He merely has the power to be the image of God and thus to be his own self, or to refuse to be God's image and to destroy the meaning of his own life.

The importance of the incarnation for human life was put in clear perspective by Vatican Council II. The *Pastoral Constitution on the Church in the Modern World* (n. 22) states that "only in the mystery of the incarnate Word does the mystery of man take on light. For Adam, the first man, was a figure of him who was to come, namely, Christ the Lord. Christ, the final Adam, by the revelation of the mystery of the Father and his love, fully reveals man to himself and makes his supreme calling clear." The reality of Christ, namely, God's self-manifestation to man in human existence and the free and autonomous response to God, contains the full revelation of man to himself. The human being, to the extent that he participates in humanity, shares in this same reality which Christ is. In his free and autonomous response to God he is a living image of God and his life becomes a continuous worship. That's why the same Pastoral Constitution (n. 43) points out that precisely the spirit of the Gospel demands a conscientious discharge of man's earthly duties and responsibilities. It adds the warning that religion does not consist in acts of worship alone and in the discharge of certain moral obligations.

In this perspective the human relationship to one's neighbor receives a very specific meaning. Kindness and goodness and justice toward the neighbor are not mere means to increase graces, but the very acts themselves can visibly express God's love in human activity. In a very concrete sense everyone can be "the seeing eye" for the blind, the strength for the lame, and health for the sick. We can be this in a concrete

physical manner, but also in a figurative manner by mutual
help and understanding. We could say that truly human
actions translate God's love into a human language. Then
in faith we can see God in the neighbor, not as a pious reflection, but in man's active, respectful and loving human
relationship with fellow men God's creative love becomes
visible and tangible.

The Church in Human Life

If the full meaning of the incarnation finds its fulfillment
in the fact that humanity becomes the living created expression of God's presence in the universe manifesting itself in
interhuman relationships, then the gathering of those who
accept this belief is the constant visible presence of God on
earth. The authentic human values which must be lived in the
world have been brought to fullness in Christ. This specific
task "is carried forward in the mission of the Holy Spirit
and through him continues in the Church in which we learn
the meaning of our terrestrial life through our faith" (*Dogmatic Constitution on the Church*, n. 48). Like any per-
manent gathering of human beings, the Church also needs
essentially an external organization, but the Church becomes
truly Church only when within this organization the profound human values are lived to their fullest extent, without
being impeded by organizational structures. The catholicity
is not to be understood primarily in terms of territorial extension, which is only a secondary meaning of it. Catholicity
is the whole world of man as person with all his human relationships. Catholicity is a vertical depth-dimension rather
than an horizontal perspective.

In our search for the meaning of God we come to the
conclusion that God is a living reality and a depth-dimension
in human existence. He is more than the creator who gave

existence to man, and different also from a judge who rewards or punishes. He is the constant source of man's being. He communicates to man an existence which finds its ultimate fulfillment in being the living manifestation of the creator himself. Whether man recognizes it or not, God is an essential dimension of his life and being, because God is precisely that aspect in the human existence which makes man fully human.

II
THE MEANING OF HUMAN LIFE

In our search for the meaning of God we had to say much about man also, since we can only know God by our human intellect and describe him in human terms. In this description we tacitly assumed that man is more than a chemical or biochemical composition. It is this point that now needs to be studied in some greater detail. Obviously man is different from a stone, a plant, or even any other kind of being. But we face a problem as soon as we try to describe in what exactly this difference exists. The differences in chromosomes and other biochemical structures don't account for man's ways of acting which make him entirely different from any kind of animal. The way humans communicate with one another by signs and language, and the manner in which they display understanding, attention, goodness, concern, tact and creativity, place them on a totally different level from any other being. Physically and biochemically, humans may perhaps fall under the same laws as animals and be classified as a particular animal species, but in their whole approach to life and in their self-expression they show themselves very different. Their manner of communicating with one another and their attitude toward their surroundings show that there is a form of life in them which surpasses the form of life of any other being on earth. Though we experience human life always in connection with material existence, we also see in it an element which not only surpasses the material reality, but which, to an extent, is the master over this reality.

The human being seems to have a foothold in two different realms, namely, in the corporeal or physical and in the spiritual. Traditionally this is expressed in the saying that man is composed of body and soul. With all due respect for tradition, this composition of "body and soul" is rather confusing. It makes one think there are two different entities in the human being, a body and a soul, which eventually can exist in their own right. This is clearly stated in the expression that in death the soul is separated from the body, and that at the end of the world soul and body will be reunited. Although it was never the intention of any teaching authority to make soul and body two separately operating sources of action in man, the practical consequences of this approach led to many inaccuracies.

Let us examine a few. We experience that the body is short-lived, and then completely disintegrates. Therefore, the real value of man doesn't lie in the body but in the soul. If the soul alone is all-important, the body is easily reduced to a mere hiding place or prison of the soul, one which in many aspects impedes its freedom and development. Then perfection or holiness (or whole-ness) can only be achieved by a flight from the world. It may easily create a tendency to disregard the material aspects of man and to consider them as a burden. Human joy and pleasure will be frowned upon as dangerous things which lead man away from God. Second, although the soul is never encountered without the body, its final perfection is supposed to lie in being without the body. This means that the human perfection is placed in a state which we cannot recognize as human in the only way we can understand this word. Furthermore, if the soul were this separate entity, a *pure* spirit which somehow is connected with a body temporarily, then their influence upon each other becomes an indissoluble problem.

For these reasons present-day thinkers tend to avoid this "body-soul" composition. The corporeal-spiritual reality of the human person is now described as one and the same entity having two *aspects* (not parts) which together make this being *human*. So the body exists only as a *human* body when and insofar as it is endowed with the spiritual qualities. The spiritual aspect is human only when and insofar as it is embodied. What man's condition will be in death and after death is beyond the scope of our present discussion. Here we are dealing with the human reality on earth which may not be dichotomized or reduced to a duality. In the human encounter we are faced with the whole human being. In every form of conversation there is much more than causing and receiving vibrations of the air. In these vibrations something is communicated when we meet as persons in authentic encounter. There is a person-to-person exchange. In the individual human being the bodily aspect necessarily influences the spiritual aspect, and vice versa. For example, a severe brain tumor may totally impair the mental capacities, and the constant fear of becoming ill greatly increases the chances of illness. In the curing of many (if not all) "physical" indispositions, the personal attitude and will to recover play an unmistakable role.

On the other hand, the corporeal and the spiritual may not be identified either. What is spiritual is by its nature beyond the grasp of the material. The spiritual by its nature cannot be encompassed by material possibilities. For the same reason it can never express itself fully in anything material. In the human encounter we meet the whole person, corporeal and spiritual, but since the corporeal can never adequately express the spiritual aspect, the same human body both reveals the presence of the person and at the same time hides the depth of the same person. In a certain way the bodily expression is always a mask of the deeper reality. The individual can use this situation to present himself as he is, at least as adequately as possible, or hide himself as much as possible and engage consciously in role-playing. For example, a friendly conversation between two politicians may be a sincere effort to bring various groups closer together, but it may also be the opportunity to discover each other's weaknesses.

The contemporary approach does not solve the mystery that man is, but at least it makes us aware of the unity which man is. Spirit and body are two aspects of the one reality which is human, but spirit and body are not the same. This same reality, which is human, at the same time is both material and transcending the material. In an effort to avoid the dichotomizing influence of terms such as soul and body, we might say that man has the aspects of "corporeity" and "intersubjectivity." [4] In this context corporeity must not be identified with the physical body. Rather it is the physical reality of man exactly insofar as it makes the *human* reality present. Intersubjectivity cannot be identified with spirit or soul, but it is that aspect of man in which he can communicate with others and through which he can grow in contact with others toward a fuller being of himself.

III
The Task of Human Life

The meaning of human life cannot be sufficiently understood without a deeper insight into the task of human life. We purposely speak about the task *of* human life and not about the human task or the task *in* human life. We want to stress that human life itself *is* a task, rather than to say that man must fulfill a task in his life. If man had to fulfill a task *in* life, he himself would be a static reality while the task would be something outside him which would not actually change his own value. If man must fulfill the task *of* his life, then his own life develops exactly in the performance of the task.

Perhaps we may try to clarify this with an example. The lioness protects and feeds her cubs. In normal circumstances this is an irresistible impulse. But once the young have grown up and the task is finished, the mother lion has not changed in individual value. The only one who has gained anything is the young. The human couple also protect and feed their children, but in the performance of this task it is not just the child that gains. Precisely in the performance of their tasks the parents themselves undergo a profound change. In normal circumstances their personality is immeasurably enriched by it. They have a new human dimension which they never had before. In a very real way they have shaped or formed or created their own life as it is now.

This example of protecting and feeding the young includes another important aspect. The mother lion does not plan the "education." She is driven by blind instinct and impulse. There may be a certain adaptation to physical circumstances, but no planning. In the human couple this is different. Normally they foresee and aim. In a more or less detailed outline they know what they want to reach, and above all they take consciously into account what possibilities they see in the child and in the circumstances of their life. They plan to let the child grow up in a way which they *consciously recognize as human.* Within certain limitations it is largely in their power to *determine* the direction. This is the aspect in which we specifically recognize the human being. Man is not only the source of his own actions in the sense that his actions come forth from his own inner source (to an extent this is also the case in animals), but he is also the master of his own activity. This means that within certain limits he himself decides on the action and determines its direction. At this point we see the deepest meaning of human life and also the meaning of God in human life. In this perspective Thomas Aquinas already said that he wanted to study man, who is the image and likeness of God, insofar as he (man) is also the source of his own activity because he has a free will and is the master of his own actions (*S.T.* I–II, Prol.).

God did not create man according to a recipe which can be found in a book, nor did he write a manual according to which the human being must develop. The creator made human life itself the "book" in which the purpose and meaning of human life can be found. He gave this "book" to us to read so that we can discover what we are. But in this same book the concrete expression of human life must be written, and he gave to us the task to write our own life story. Man must write his own reading and read his own writing.

Earlier we have said that our knowledge of God is taken from our understanding of human reality. We encounter man in his actual situation. He is material, yet he transcends his material existence. He experiences that he is the master of his own actions, yet he knows also that by doing certain things he enriches himself as a person and by doing other things he decreases his own personal value. He realizes that in his life there is a purpose which he has to fulfill, otherwise he is not really himself. The purpose itself is not of his own making, but he has the task to discover this purpose in the total circumstances of his own life and to translate it into a concrete reality in daily living.

While giving a concrete expression to his own being, man realizes that he himself is not the source of his being, or of his being in this specific way. There is a power behind him which escapes his human management and comprehension— a power on which he is totally dependent, yet which makes itself known and understood in his own human approach to life, or to the task of his life. Man's own goodness expresses the goodness of the One-behind-him; man's failure is the denial of the manifestation of the One-behind-him. But just as man knows himself to be responsible for the fulfillment of the self-manifestation of the divine, he also knows himself to be responsible for the non-fulfillment of this self-manifestation.

In this light we may be able to see that the goal of man's existence is at the same time immanent and transcendent. By immanent we mean that man has the task to develop in such a way that he does justice to the potential which is in him. He must become himself as a human being. He has fulfilled himself if he is the best human being he can be in view of the circumstances of his life. But within all this is a transcendent goal, because man is not the source of his own being. Since he is not the source of his own being he reflects necessarily the One who indeed is the source of his being as man. Here is a goal that goes beyond the immanent goal of human self-realization, but this goal finds its fulfillment only to the extent that the human self-realization corresponds to man's actual possibilities and demands in the total setting of his life. All this is terribly abstract.

Perhaps the following example might help to make this clearer. The musician has expressed his deeper and inner feelings in a piece of music. The more perfectly the pianist brings this music to life, the more correctly he expresses the personality and feelings of the composer. The music contains the possibility to reflect the deepest and inmost self of the musician, but it has to be brought to life before it actually makes this inmost person perceptible. In a similar way does man contain the self-manifestation of the creator, but it has to be brought to life in the concrete expression of his human existence. Thus his self-fulfillment is the attainment of his transcendent goal. This human self-fulfillment is accomplished by the development of the full way of living *as the human being is* in his corporeal-spiritual existence, or in his corporeity and intersubjectivity. These are two aspects of the same reality, so that corporeity is intersubjective, and intersubjectivity can express itself in this world only in (physical) corporeity. This gives a special perspective and meaning to the human activity. Everything that man does has a special depth-dimension precisely because he is human. Even in material activities such as walking or eating, etc., the action performed by man can be on a totally different level from the same actions performed by an animal, because in man it is an expression of self-determination, while in an animal it is a biochemical and/or instinctive reaction. The fact that man is a "person" makes every comparison of the value of his actions with similar actions of animals totally invalid.

Nor can it be maintained that man, because he has intellect and free will, can know the laws of biological and biochemical nature and that he then must follow them on his own responsibility. If the fulfillment of man consists in the perfect fulfillment of biological laws, then his dignity does not go beyond the level of biological dignity either. Man must make himself ever more human in the totality of his condition, i.e., in his corporeity and in his intersubjectivity. For example, the love relationship between man and woman must be exactly what it says, a love relationship. That this relationship expresses itself in biological structures does not mean that biological structures dominate the relationship. They are only a co-constituent element in the relationship between human beings, but they can never outline the ultimate value, for in man their value is totally different from the value which similar actions have in animals. In intersubjectivity, human actions receive their proper value and meaning. Man develops in relation with the world around him, especially in relation with other human beings.

Vatican Council II expresses this very clearly when the *Pastoral Constitution on the Church in the Modern World* states: "For by his innermost nature man is a social being, and unless he relates himself to others he can neither live nor develop his potential" (n. 12). It is then in the interhuman relationship that man becomes his real self and that he fulfills the purpose of his own being. In this same relationship also, his relationship to God receives a concrete expression as we read in St. John: "By this love you have for one another, everyone will know that you are my disciples" (1 Jn. 13:35), and "Anyone who says, 'I love God,' and hates his brother, is a liar, since a man who does not love the brother whom he can see cannot love God whom he has never seen" (1 Jn. 4:20). Without going into detailed description of the meaning of this love, we may say that this includes the giving of self to the other for the creative development of the human situation and happiness, while in this self-giving the agent becomes a more human and a better human being himself.

The whole material world and all human capacities obtain their value from this specific relationship. So riches, culture and power, honor, fame and pleasure are only co-constituents of the human self-expression. They are the external and material form of the human self-expression in this human world, the way through which he influences his surroundings and through which he is influenced by his surroundings. In themselves they can never constitute the human fulfillment or happiness, but only to the extent that they contribute to the betterment of interhuman relationships in which the living God becomes visibly present in human existence.

Now we can turn again to the question whether we need God to live the fullness of human life. Again we must make a distinction. The avowed atheist will deny this need. He will see the transcendent aspect of his existence in the betterment of the human family, without trying to explain the deepest desires of man. On the other hand, if we do accept the existence of God, the answer to our question will be a very definite yes. We can see God as the ultimate source of existence who in continuous self-communication gives "being itself" and "being in this specific way" to creation. In giving "being in this specific way," the purpose of the individual existing creature has been given, so that the creature can be himself only if it fulfills this specific way of being. For man this includes existence in corporeity and in intersubjectivity—to be the source and the master of his own activity in responsible self-realization. But this becoming of man himself must take place in this world in an interhuman relationship, visibly expressed in his corporeal existence. Then God is not an outsider in human existence, nor is he a superfluous luxury. The contrary is true. The existence of God lies at the core of the human being. God's immanence and transcendence make man what he is. When speaking about human life we may say with Franco Crespi:

> I start from the premise that I regard the relationship with God as a constitutive dimension of human existence, in such a way that it cannot be eluded even by those who are unaware of it or do not recognize it, since it forms part of the existential situation of man, or rather, it is the term that primarily found the sense of the existence itself.[5]

NOTES

1. Ignace Lepp, *Atheism in Our Time* (Macmillan, New York, 1963), p. 7.
2. *Ibid.*, p. 17.
3. Bruce Vawter, "The God of the Bible," in *God, Jesus, Spirit,* ed. Daniel Callahan (Herder and Herder, New York, 1969), p. 16.
4. William van der Marck, *Toward a Christian Ethic* (Newman Press, New York, 1967), pp. 21–28.
5. Franco Crespi, "The Process of Secularization: From Desacralization to Religion," in *IDO-C*, 68–9, p. 3.

III
Performing the Human Task in a Human Way

In our concern whether or not there is any need for God in human life, we came to the conclusion that God does not just have a place in human life, but that he is the core of human life itself. The contingency of human existence makes us accept that man's existence is the continuous self-manifestation or self-communication of God who makes his own inner being perceptible in humanity. Therefore, the more deeply human (we mean human in its constructive personal and interpersonal dimensions) man lives his life, the clearer God's created self-manifestation will be. The more man is really himself, the more he transcends himself, and reversely, the more self-seeking he is, the less human he will be, and the less he will manifest God's presence and purpose in the human world. Our concern about God-in-human-life must, therefore, coincide with the concern about the performance of the human task.

The Essential Unity of the Human Task

It has been the irony of religious approach during many centuries that an unbalanced stress was placed upon the value of "elevating our heart to God" or "offering one's work to God" or "renewing one's intention," etc. Not that there is anything wrong if a person does those things. On the contrary, it is beautiful. The sad part is that we often did (and perhaps still do) look upon those things as a sign of being "close to God." This made the person who lived in the quiet setting of a convent and sighed a host of ejaculatory prayers much holier than the mother of a large family who had no time for such things. Thank goodness, this norm of evaluation has largely disappeared.

However, the underlying concept has often not disappeared. It is still not uncommon to consider human activity as a composite of many more or less independent elements. The corporeal or material element in the human action is then sharply distinguished from the spiritual element. We say, then, that what makes an action really human is that it is performed with knowledge and free will. There is a tendency to overlook the fact that the spiritual aspect is very much present in the corporeal aspect, and that the spiritual aspect can never be realized without a corporeal dimension. Intellectual activity is greatly influenced by physical dispositions, especially by the condition of the brains, while the will is, among other things, closely connected with the nervous system. In speaking about human activity and human task we must be careful not to elevate the intellect and will to the status of independent realities, but we should see them and treat them as aspects of the human *totality*.

Especially the will used to be assigned an extremely important and almost autonomous status as a "humanizing factor" in human action. In his recent book *Love and Will*, Rollo May gives an interesting description of the role which the Victorian age ascribed to free will and will power. They were used to manipulate man's surrounding and man himself, thus reducing man himself to an object.[1] Reason and free will used to be considered in an abstract way as if they existed in themselves. Consequently, all the normal human conditions such as ignorance, inadvertence, strong inclinations (passion), etc., were considered as impediments to the intellect or will. It was a rather dichotomizing approach, to which the moralists clung rigorously, but which was rejected by most other sciences. Perhaps Erich Fromm in his *Man for Himself* judges too harshly when he says that this position ignores the fact that ideas and truth do not exist outside and independent of man, and that man's mind is influenced by his body, his mental state by his physical and social existence.[2] But undoubtedly there is some truth to it.

This glorification of intellect and free will was more an expression of the thinking current some centuries ago than a doctrine of Christianity. St. Thomas Aquinas saw the matter differently. He said that while irrational creatures are guided by the blind forces of laws of nature and instincts, man strives for his ultimate fulfillment by knowing and loving God (*S.T.* I–II, 1, 7). He doesn't speak of independent powers, but of the specific human way of expressing himself. This same idea we find expressed in Vatican Council II when it says that man by his interior qualities outstrips the whole sum of mere things. When man recognizes in himself a spiritual and immortal soul, he is not being mocked by a fantasy born only of physical or social influences, but is rather laying hold of the proper truth of the matter (*Pastoral Constitution on the Church in the Modern World*, n. 14). Here the Council's attention goes to the integrated human reality in which the corporeal and spiritual aspects form one unit of operation.

This unity expresses the tendency of our contemporary understanding of man. The bodily conditions and circumstances are as much part of the human action as are intellect and will, just as the body is as much part of man as is the spirit. Bodily conditions are not simply externally added limitations to human action, but inherent to the human activity itself. It is in the light of this essential unity of the human being that we want to study the performance of the human task. First we will consider man's power of self-determination within the conditioned setting of human reality. We may call this human freedom. Then we will focus upon the aspect of interpersonal response-ability, or the essential human necessity of communicating with others. Further we will see that this interpersonal relationship is by its nature constructive or destructive for the total human development and consequently good or evil. Finally we will try to place this still abstract understanding in the concrete corporeity of the human inclinations, emotions and passions. One of the advantages of this approach is that we can see from the very beginning how closely these four points are interwoven. When we speak about one individual point, the other three are present in it, even without being mentioned.

The Human Power of Self-Determination

Instead of the term "power of self-determination," we could have used the word "freedom." It is not our intention to eliminate the word "freedom," but to avoid the unfortunate connotations which are too often attached to it. In what we might call the Victorian understanding of freedom, one usually thinks of free will and will power. This will power is then seen as a special quality by which a human being can control the various inclinations, emotions and expressions of his life and behavior. For example, the foreman at a factory who gets easily impatient can control his scolding and cursing if he simply decides to develop his will power and control himself. The young couple who are looking forward to marriage have no excuse for engaging in premarital relations; they should have enough will power and use it.

When we look closely, we see that in this approach it is not the human being in his total existence who is the master and source of his activity, but one specific human quality becomes the all-important source of the human action. All the other human qualities are at best means or obstacles to the full exercise of this freedom. This means that freedom is not considered as an aspect of the integral human totality, but as an independent reality in charge of man. Contemporary philosophy, psychology and other human sciences have come to the conclusion that this understanding of freedom is largely inaccurate.

For most people there is no doubt that each individual person is responsible for his own actions. This means that each individual feels that, somehow, his own action is the result of a personal decision. He is the master of it. Often he could have done otherwise, yet he decided to act this way. Usually the decision was made not because of some unknown irresistible inner force, but because of the convergence of all kinds of circumstances which made him see that he could be himself more completely by acting in this way. It was not a fight of the will against the rest of his personality, but it was rather a decision to be-in-this-way or be-in-another-way. In the decision-making the real concern was not the realization of an abstract ideal, but the actualization of a concrete possibility of being.

Some examples may clarify what is meant. Let us say that a man on top of a high building has to go down as quickly as possible. He knows that his hands and arms are not sufficient equipment for flying and that no will power can make up for this insufficiency. His decision will be to use either the stairs or the elevator. It is not a matter of will power but of concrete self-realization. He could have jumped to the ground if he had willed to, but this would have meant self-destruction.

Another example is that of a compulsive masturbator. He feels terribly guilty about it. It doesn't even bring him real joy or satisfaction. Still, he doesn't seem able to break his habit. It is easy (but very ineffective) to say that he must rely on free will and will power to overcome this habit. Deep within the structure of his personality something is off balance. Perhaps it is a matter of repression of strong aggressive tendencies; possibly it is a reaction against deep frustrations or some other maladjustment. Then the masturbation might be the only way he sees to keep himself sane and sound insofar as circumstances allow this.

What we want to point out is that human freedom is very limited. It can express itself only within the limitations of the physiological, biological, biochemical, psychological and sociological conditions of this specific individual. We do not mean to imply that a human action is simply a necessary consequence of such conditions. But these conditions are essential elements of the human reality, and if man is the master of his own activity, then he cannot determine himself *outside* these conditions. His corporeal aspect is as essentially human as his spiritual aspect.

It would be inaccurate to consider these conditions as limitations or impediments to the human freedom. If we would see them as impediments, we would again introduce a dichotomy into the human reality. We should rather see them as the content or the sphere within which man is able to give expression to his own self in concrete reality. They are the circumscription within which the human ability of self-determination is contained. Outside this circumscription or without this circumscription no self-determination is possible. They are not an impediment but rather a co-constituent element of human freedom.

Thus far we have concentrated mainly on the individual isolated person. However, no man is an island. The human being is essentially a social being. He is somehow connected with others, not only in his origin, but also in his development and in his continued existence. Others enter into our lives with or without our free choice. In any event they must be taken into account in the decisions we make. Let us give a few examples. The married person has the ability to make love to other persons, but this action would be very destructive to the one-to-one-bond in love which is an essential aspect of marriage. Marriage is not a limitation of his free and full self-giving, but it is the sphere and circumscription within which alone his full self-determination in love is possible. One who enters a train and finds all seats taken may have the physical ability to remove a weaker person forcibly, but respect for the dignity of others makes it necessary for him to accept the prior claim of those who are already there. Again, we should not see this as a limitation of freedom but rather as a sphere for constructive self-determination.

In a certain way it is obviously correct to say that all the examples indicate limitations for men. However, these limitations are not external or accidental impositions upon an infinite freedom. On the contrary, they belong essentially to *human* freedom since they constitute the concrete reality for the constructive self-determination of the person. Disregard of this reality would make the person less human. It would be a loss of self-determination.

In this context one may be able to see that it is wrong to confuse freedom of choice with the concept of human freedom itself. Human freedom itself may be described as the specific characteristic or ability of man through which he can determine himself in such a way that his life-expression becomes meaningful for himself and for his fellow men. This ability of self-determination certainly includes the possibility of expressing oneself contrary to a constructive self-actualization. This too is a self-determination, even if it leads to a distortion of one's *human* abilities.

What we want to convey is that freedom is not an unlimited power of man which is curtailed by corporeal and psychological conditions, but is a very modest aspect of the human totality. In *A Theology for Radical Politics* Michael Novak describes freedom as "seized from within." [3] He sees it as a matter of developing one's own inner life, of becoming awake to one's own decisions, and of exercising these with greater consciousness.

This inner development is achieved by an integrating power which coordinates man's experiences and insights into one unit of operation. Man evaluates his potential not only according to its inner meaning and possibilities, but also insofar as this potential transcends its own inner structures and enters into a relationship with other beings. The sculptor who is a real master in his trade integrates in his product not only his own skill but also his knowledge of the quality and possibilities of his material. He has an understanding of the message which he wants to convey to others, and he has some insight into what this message can mean for his fellow man. These and many other factors fuse together into one act of self-determination which not only activates the sculptor's own way of being, but transcends his own individual qualities in a constructive contribution to the development of others. It is a self-determination in view of the overall circumstances of his life.[4]

We are here primarily concerned with the ethical meaning of freedom, but social and physical freedom are also implied. The prisoner doesn't have the ability to walk around wherever he wants, but he does have the ability of self-determination within the concrete circumstances of his life. Despite his limitations, the essence of freedom remains. The freedom of the millionaire is not unlimited either. His constructive self-determination is also bound to his life-situation, though his field of possibilities is much wider.

Even the traditional division of freedom into "freedom of," "freedom from" and "freedom for" makes more sense if we see them as various aspects of the human condition. "Freedom of" indicates that the agent is not determined by a specific direction, as, for instance, freedom of choice. "Freedom from" tells us that the agent is not subject to a certain force, e.g., freedom from sin. "Freedom for" shows the ability to determine oneself into a certain direction, e.g., freedom for God.

If freedom can express itself constructively only in the totality of the human situation, it is obvious that intellectual knowledge is most intimately connected with human freedom. Actually, the very word "self-determination" implies knowledge. The word "determination" always implies a conscious direction, which means knowledge. The more we know, the better we will be able to determine our direction. The better we know the laws of space, gravity, etc., the more we will be able to explore areas beyond our planet. The more man knows about his own psyche, the better he will be able to understand and direct his own way of acting, even if this would indicate many more limitations than he would like to accept. Knowledge of his restrictions increases his ability of successful self-determination, although it decreases the field of prudent experimentation.

In this light we get also a better understanding of the circumstances which were traditionally called the impediments of human freedom, such as force, fear, ignorance and passion. These are conditions of the human realm of self-determination. There is no need to go into a detailed study of each of these factors, but a few words may be said about each. (For a deeper study we may refer to van der Marck's *Toward a Christian Ethic.*[5])

"Force" is the urging into a certain direction, either from without or from within; thus it gives a new dimension to man's *ability* to determine himself, but it does not take away the ability to determine oneself *within these circumstances*. It is only within this dimension that man is responsible.

"Fear" is the knowledge, real or imaginary, of a danger, a suffering or harm connected with a certain self-expression. The understanding of the danger and the gravity of the danger, the possibility of avoiding it, the need to perform this action, etc.—all this again is a condition of the human ability of self-determination. It is not as if force and fear have no impact upon human freedom, but they are not *outside* the human freedom. They are *inherent* to this specific self-determination. Let us remember that freedom and self-determination do not exist in a vacuum but only in concrete human reality.

If force and fear influence the operational field of human self-determination by barring a certain area either by force or by threat, so passion influences this same operational field by pulling into a certain direction. The strength of an internal inclination or the attraction of an object brightens a certain form of self-realization to such an extent that the advisability or even the possibility of other forms is no longer understood.

In an entirely different way the range of human self-determination is influenced by "ignorance." Earlier we have said that self-determination presupposes a certain amount of knowledge. Where there is no knowledge, self-determination simply cannot exist. On the other hand, the more complete human knowledge is, the better man will be able to determine the direction of his life. Thus the important question is not only how much knowledge a person actually has, but also how much knowledge can be expected reasonably in a person in this specific condition. Here the importance of inadvertence and negligence becomes evident.

In this perspective we see, then, that human freedom unfolds itself as a specific aspect of the whole human reality. To take this freedom out of context and to raise it to the dignity of an autonomous and independent quality would mean to introduce an unreal and inaccurate division in the human totality. This would lead to untrue and unrealistic moral evaluations.

The human self-realization is always to a certain degree connected with other persons. A closer examination of this specific point may give us a better insight in the meaning of the human ability of self-determination.

Interpersonal Response-Ability

The nature of human existence in this world demands that man be in continuous contact with his fellow creatures who share this universe with him. Man is part of this world, and whether he likes it or not there is a mutual influence between the individual himself and the world outside him. Man needs the material world. He needs to breathe and to feed himself. Man needs to cultivate the earth in order to reach a reasonably comfortable living. In a very concrete way man puts his own stamp on the material world. But the material world puts its stamp on man as well. A moderate climate and a fertile geographical region have a very different influence upon human development than the hardship of a blazing desert or the rigors of sub-zero climatic conditions.

This form of mutual influence is totally different from the mutual exchange between human beings. Man imposes himself upon the material world. He controls temperature by developing systems for heating or air conditioning. He controls the fertility of the land by building canals for irrigation or draining. Man adapts to nature, at least to a certain extent, and he adapts nature to himself. In this process, man is the active element which has the ability to respond without being necessitated by blind laws. Though man remains subject to the laws of physical nature, his power of adaptation comes forth from an inner source of which he is the master. He exercises this power by subjecting the material world to himself.

In his encounter with the world outside himself, however, he meets other beings who have the same dignity as he has, and who respond to the material world in the same way as he does. It is in the recognition and respect for others of equal dignity that the truly human values develop. By contact with them, man gains not only strength and skill and health, but also an understanding of what he is himself. He gains an awareness of his own dignity. He desires to be respected by others as he respects them. This mutual exchange is experienced as an enhancement of dignity and increase of happiness.

Human interdependence has its physical and biological aspects. Man is born from other human beings. To sustain and develop life demands a long and constant care. But beyond these physical and biological aspects lies another field of communication which transcends biology. The gestation period and the birth of the child have an influence upon the parents which is completely different from that which similar happenings have on other creatures. The encounter between the growing child and the mother and the world has an impact upon all who are involved. It is a formative influence which creates attitudes. It goes far beyond the bodily aspect of existence. It is the mutual experience of the corporeal-*spiritual* unit which is the human person.

In the human person there is a quality through which the individual necessarily influences others and is influenced by others beyond the biological or biophysical level. Because of this mutual influence, the person develops in a certain direction. This mutual giving and receiving is totally unconscious and beyond personal control during the early stages of life, but subsequent maturation brings it partly under human control. It then becomes one of the most important elements in human self-determination. This relationship which expresses itself in and through the biological, but which goes far beyond the biological, is in a true sense a person-to-person relationship.

The quality that enables men to produce this necessary mutual interchange we call the "interpersonal response-ability," because it enables man to give a person-to-person response. We use this term to indicate the specific spiritual aspect of the human being without pulling the spirit out of the human context. With van der Marck[6] and others, one may call this "intersubjectivity," but in our opinion "intersubjectivity" refers to the result rather than to the basic quality itself; therefore, we prefer the term "interpersonal response-ability." This helps us also to stay away from any moral judgment at this moment. Every interhuman relationship has necessarily an ethical or moral value, since it increases or impedes the human development in some way or another. But this is a topic for later study. Here we want to focus our attention on this interpersonal response-ability itself. We see the involvement of the whole person in almost all the circumstances of life.

Let us consider a few evident examples. If one person shoots another to death, we have a person-to-person relationship. The one responded to the other. The physical effect is the same in every case of this kind, namely the death of one, but the interpersonal relationship can cover a wide variety of possibilities. The killer may have acted toward the other as a defender of justice (capital punishment), as a protector of his own life (self-defense), or to add force to his infringement upon the rights of others (holdup with murder). Many other possibilities could be mentioned, but all would be variations of an interpersonal response. All explain how in a particular case one person relates to the other. The kind of human response determines the human value that the action has. This should make it clear that the physical or material result which we see must never be mistaken for the *human* action. The human action as human is only understood when we know how the ability to respond was activated in relation to the other.

The human response is always and exclusively given in the context of a human situation. The totality alone—the response in the context of the situation—constitutes the human action. Every human action has, of course, always many "circumstances," but these circumstances should not be considered as factors *added* to the action. The circumstances are nothing more or less than the context in which the human response manifests itself. To give an example of what we mean, let us consider the much debated issue of abortion. At this point we wish to abstain from any moral evaluation, but to focus our attention exclusively on what is going on as inter-human response.

Let us consider these cases. Mrs. X., a mother of five, has a uterine disease which prevents the uterus from forming its proper lining during pregnancy. The wall of the uterus is so thin that any progressed form of fetal development will rupture the uterus and cause death to herself and the unborn child. Despite her desire to carry this pregnancy to the end, her concern for her own life and for the well-being of her family leaves her only one choice—abortion.

Mrs. Y. has the Rh blood-factor. Her first child died after birth, the second was severely retarded, the third (a girl) survived and seems quite normal. She has had two miscarriages. Medical indications leave no reasonable doubt that her present pregnancy will end in a child with very severe brain damage, if it will survive at all. The emotional strain of the past, the grim prospect for the future and the great financial drain caused by the necessary institutional care for the one retarded child drive her to such a state of despair that she sees only one solution—abortion.

Mrs. Z. finds her greatest delight in parties and social entertaining. Her present pregnancy is most unwelcome since it will mean a severe handicap to what she wants in life. She decides on an easy way out—abortion.

We have classified these three cases under one common denominator—abortion—because all the ladies chose the same way to attain their goal at this stage of their life, namely, the removal of a non-viable fetus. But in terms of human response we see three totally different realities. Mrs. X. displays a deep concern for her own life. This concern is not just for selfish reasons, but it is inspired by the love for her husband and children to whom she feels that she has a serious obligation. It is a deeply human concern in which the individual tries to contribute constructively to the well-being of humanity as far as this is within her reach. Mrs. Y. is concerned about her own sanity, her mental balance, the happiness of the husband and the little family which has been given to her. She knows what misery will lie in store if the pregnancy continues, and she is also convinced that past circumstances have drained her strength. She sees only one constructive approach for herself and others. Mrs. Z.'s concern is purely centered around herself and her pleasures. Even the life of the unborn child is not sacred enough to be permitted to interfere with her own wishes.

It would be incorrect to say that the circumstances "have changed the moral value" of the action in each of these cases. There is not merely a change in moral value, but there are three totally different *human* actions insofar as they are *human*. The material result is the same, of course, but the material result does not constitute the *human* action. It is the interpersonal response which gives the action its human value. The circumstances are not merely additional or accidental elements to the action of abortion, but they are inherent to the *human* action. The circumstances are the context within which alone the human and interpersonal aspect of the action finds its concrete realization. They are the perceptible description of the human dimension which the material action has. In these circumstances the interpersonal response-ability is brought to full human activation.

Most important among the circumstances is the relationship between the "means" and the "end." Too often we see the means and the end in their material, individual and separate appearance. We treat them and we evaluate them as independent things. In the cases of Mmes. X, Y, and Z, we are inclined to see the removal of the non-viable fetus as the means, and we place this in juxtaposition to the end, which in these cases varies from deep human concern for life and humanity to selfish pleasure seeking. This approach seems very inaccurate. The human action possesses a special unity and uniqueness (cf. the author's study "The Principle of Double Effect").[7] The human action is performed in space and time and consequently has a succession of elements. But even if the material parts do not coincide in this sequence of space and time, we may not consider them independently from each other. The simple reason is that they do not exist independently.

An example may serve to clarify this point. When a surgical team performs a heart transplant, there is a bewildering amount of successive activities. To mention only a few, the heart of the donor is excised, as is that of the recipient, the donor's heart is implanted, the transplanted heart is reactivated, and many other steps are taken for the cure of the recipient. None of these different steps exists without all the others. Abstractly we can say, of course, that a surgeon can excise the healthy heart from a deceased person and the diseased heart from a living person. But the concrete human action exists only in reality and not in the abstract. As a human reality—that is, as an interhuman response or as the activation of the interpersonal response-ability—the implantation and cure are already contained in the excision of both hearts, just as the excision is contained in the implantation and cure.

The same material reality can be the recipient of many different human responses. This should make us understand that we may never attach a specific human meaning to an "abstract" material expression. If we see a young lady crying, we do not know whether she has lost her boyfriend, her mother or her diamond ring, or whether she has hurt her foot or perhaps has a toothache. When a non-viable fetus is removed from the uterus, it may be an expression of deep human concern or selfish disregard for human life. The material result is open to receive many different human responses.

Accordingly, in every human action the end enters into the means and gives them its human meaning, and the means enter into the end and translate the human meaning into a concrete reality. The human value of an action can only be understood if we keep looking at the totality of the action, and within this totality we must try to see all the different parts in their proper place.

So far we have considered the human task of self-determination, and we have tried to show that this task can only be fulfilled because of the specific human ability of interpersonal response in which one person relates to the other as a person. We abstained, however, from speaking about any moral evaluation, because this demands much more than looking at the human response-ability. It includes, among other things, the relation of man to his fellow man. This moral aspect we will study more closely now in the following pages.

The Moral Perspective

Under the heading of "moral perspective" we will try to describe a third aspect of human self-realization, namely, whether or not a specific action is a constructive or harmful contribution to this self-realization. Traditionally this specific aspect would be studied as the question whether an action is good or evil. With all respect for this traditional approach, such a division of human actions into good or evil is too easily conceived as an "either-or" issue: the human action is seen either as good or as evil. In every human action, however, so many constructive and harmful aspects are inextricably interwoven that it is often almost impossible to qualify the action in one word. That's why we would rather speak of the moral perspective. In this way we have an opportunity to look at the whole of human reality; we can look at the action as an expression of man as a corporeal-spiritual being. The moral perspective wants to look at the human action precisely insofar as it is *human*. An action is human only when it is a self-determination in the human ability to respond as a person to the outside world of men and things.

A few pages ago we indicated that the material result may never be identified with the human perspective. In the example of abortion we emphasized that the removal of the non-viable fetus is open to many different human meanings. Only when this human meaning is taken into consideration does it become possible to establish what kind of human action there is. Only the *human* action is open to a moral evaluation. In ordinary conversation people are very much inclined to put a name-tag of good or evil on material results. For example, they find it a "bad thing" if an arm or leg is amputated and a "bad effect" when the fetus dies in the surgical removal of an ectopic pregnancy.

What they really mean in such circumstances is that man's bodily integrity or human life has suffered a loss. In many cases, however, we are ready to accept that this loss is a necessary though most unfortunate result of human limitations. We would prefer to preserve bodily integrity, but the amputation was the only way to preserve the human life. We would prefer to preserve the life of the fetus, but its removal is the only way to preserve at least the life of the mother. Because of this human meaning which the preservation of life has, we are accustomed to call the whole human action good; it is in its totality constructive for the well-being of the individual and of human society. Accordingly, in making a moral evaluation of a human action it is not merely the material result which is decisive, nor is it merely the intention of the agent, since the intention only establishes the human meaning of the action. It is this reality of the human action together with its impact upon the well-being of the individual and the human society which is the norm for moral evaluation.

Traditionally the foundation for moral evaluation was seen to be in three sources, namely, the object, the circumstances and the end. We have tried to show that circumstances and end are aspects of the human meaning and do not exist autonomously. The object of the action is the material reality. This is certainly a very important aspect of the human action, but in itself it has no human value. In all fairness to the traditional approaches of moral theology, we must add that by the "object" the moralists meant the "moral object" of the action. This qualification meant that a number of circumstances were included in the "object." Nevertheless, their way of speaking led to the custom of calling certain actions always and everywhere sinful, or, as they used to say, "evil in themselves"—for example, the direct killing of an innocent human being or the use of contraceptive means. The qualification "evil in itself" was too often ascribed to the material result itself without the interpersonal perspective.

Let us consider again the example of the direct killing of an innocent human being. No self-respecting moralist holds that one may not kill an attacker if this is the only way to save one's own life, even if the attacker is completely insane. Now, the insane person is just as innocent as an unborn child. To say that the attacker was acting "illegitimately" does not hold, because "illegitimacy" in an action presupposes responsibility, and the insane attacker has no responsibility. Therefore, the principle that one is never allowed directly to kill an innocent human being has no *absolute* value.

Another element or perspective is required to evaluate the morality of this action, namely, the interpersonal aspect of the human self-realization. In the killing of a human being, the issue is not whether the person who is going to be killed is guilty or innocent, nor whether the killing is direct or indirect; the question, rather, is what kind of human self-realization is taking place and what is the interpersonal impact of this action.

The same line of thought must be used in evaluating the use of contraceptives. The important question in such cases is not whether there is an interference in biological structures, but what kind of person-to-person relationship is expressed. There is no doubt, however, that biological structures are an important aspect of the interpersonal relationship. In a recent publication *God's Love in Human Language. A Study of the Meaning of Marriage and Conjugal Responsibility*,[8] we have worked out in greater depth what an interpersonal relationship in marriage means. We may refer the reader to this work for a deeper appreciation of this perspective.

Accordingly, we can never maintain in general terms that certain human actions are always evil, "evil in themselves." Only when the human meaning and the interpersonal impact enter into the evaluation can an action be called good or evil. Individual actions can be good or evil, but it is theologically incorrect to call a certain action, such as the direct killing of an innocent person, an "evil in itself." Evil doesn't exist in itself, but in the reality of personal self-determination with its interpersonal repercussions. It is in this context alone that an action can be evaluated as good or evil.

All this, however, does not mean that a general qualification as good or evil is completely meaningless. The material result is always the visible and perceptible way in which the self-realization and interpersonal response is made manifest. Hence the killing of a human being is always a serious matter in interhuman relations; moreover, it is a most unfortunate event and implies that most probably there exists a personal or interhuman deficiency. This is what should be expressed and understood by the term "evil in itself." At the same time the possibility that the action may have another human meaning and interpersonal influence should not be categorically excluded.

This brings up the point of the "means" and the "end." One often hears that we may never use evil means to reach a good result or end. From the preceding considerations, it should be clear that means and end don't exist as independent things. In his book *Man for Himself*, Erich Fromm points out that means and end refer to the same reality but from a different point of view. When we speak about the means, we look at the action from its beginning or from some point in the series of events which constitute the whole action. When we speak about the end we look at the same action, but now at its point of fulfillment.[9]

If, for instance, we consider a heart transplant, we can look at the excision of a heart as the means, but its implantation into the recipient has entered into the excision giving it its human meaning. On the other hand, the excision enters into the end (implantation), for instance, insofar as it is very important whether the donor is a deceased or a living person. The means, therefore, may never be evaluated in terms of its own *material* structure, but only in connection with its human meaning. So also the end may never be evaluated on its own abstract merits, but only in its concrete expression in the means. It is only in the totality of the human action that the interpersonal importance can become evident. We must, therefore, say that there are no such things as means "which are evil in themselves." What doesn't exist in itself cannot have any meaning in itself. It is only because of the end that the means become meaningful.

We are not implying that the end sanctifies the means, but only that the end gives the human meaning to the means. Only on this basis can we start to evaluate the human action as a whole. Since the means are the concrete circumscription within which the human action is materialized, they are a most important element in the evaluation of the interpersonal relationship. If, for example, we want to escape an attack, we may try this by a disarming smile, by running away, or by killing the attacker. Each of these possibilities has a totally different effect as an interpersonal response. How exactly one activates one's ability to give the correct interpersonal response must be based upon what is in fact most constructive or least harmful for the interpersonal expression.

Immediately connected with the study of means and end is the problem of human actions which allegedly have a double effect, one good and one evil. In our essay on "The Principle of Double Effect" we have elaborated on this point. Without going into great detail here, we may briefly state that this problem is based upon false premises. For many years one of the classical examples for this principle of double effect has been the removal of a tubal pregnancy. The good effect is the saving of the mother's life; the evil effect is the death of the fetus. Both results flow forth from the same human action. Both results were seen as happenings which had to be considered separately, and since both results were seen as separate effects of a human action, they were evaluated independently. The traditional reasoning used to be that the removal of the fetus was the killing of human life, but this same removal was also the saving of human life, namely, of the mother. It became a weighing of life against life. One considered each of the two effects in their material setting on an independent scale of human values, as if one effect could exist apart from the other.

This is precisely what we call "false premises." The removal of the tubal fetus was the means which received its human meaning from the end. The removal of the fetus and the cure of the mother are two *material* effects but NOT two *human* effects. There is only one human effect, namely, the cure of the mother. Whether or not this is an acceptable human action depends on what it means as an interhuman response.

A few decades ago, when it was discovered that a tubal pregnancy was a disease because of the wrong location of the fetus, moralists concluded that the "diseased" part of the fallopian tube could be removed even if it contained the fetus. The killing of the fetus was now reduced to an "indirect" killing which would be acceptable for very serious reasons. This is pure semantics and self-deception. The humanizing element in the action is the cure of the mother which can be achieved only by the removal of the fetus. Whether this removal is done with or without a piece of the fallopian tube does not change the *human* value. It is not the fallopian tube which endangers the mother's life, but the tubal fetus. It is not the removal of the affected part of the tube which cures the mother but the removal of the ectopic fetus. To say that it would be immoral to remove the fetus from the tube, while it would be morally permissible to remove the fetus *with the affected part* of the tube, would mean to place the ultimate moral evaluation on a purely material level. Here again we do not have two human effects, but only one, and the material condition by itself may never form the basis for moral evaluation. In the human meaning of the action—the cure of the mother in and through the death of the fetus—it will be necessary to discover the interhuman value of the total action.

Although it may seem that we have gone slightly off our topic, we feel that we must point to another important aspect. When people speak about the value and dignity of human life, they are inclined to look at the individual life of the individual person. One certainly must have the deepest respect for the life of the individual, but one must not forget that no individual is an island by himself alone. The value of human life is directly connected with other persons. People accept this connection in the evaluation of legitimate self-defense. It is precisely because of interpersonal relationships and the protection of the individual and society that people admit the morality of self-defense. Here the value of the individual human being is placed in an interpersonal perspective. Why, then, should one hesitate to apply the same principle to the situation of tubal pregnancy or other circumstances where human life is involved?

Going back to the principle of double effect, we see then

that this double effect doesn't really exist. Obviously, there are two or more material results. Since these material results in themselves do not have a human meaning until the end has entered into the action, this action cannot receive a moral evaluation either. A moral evaluation refers to the human action precisely insofar as it is human. But the principle of double effect speaks precisely about one human action which by its very nature can receive only one human evaluation. It is clear that in our approach to the issue we must abandon many of the certain answers which used to be given in the past. This is also why we speak about the moral perspective rather than about good and evil deeds, for in this way we can look at the human totality without being prejudiced.

Throughout the preceding paragraphs we have repeatedly referred to the human totality, but we always included in this the bodily dimension of the human being. The study of this bodily aspect, too, is essential if we want to understand what it means to perform the human task in a human way.

The Human Task in Man's Bodily Dimension

Man's ability to determine himself or to be the source and master of his own activity, man's ability to respond on an interpersonal level, and ultimately the evaluation as to whether this self-expression is constructive or harmful for the human totality—all these aspects lack the concrete individuality of man unless they find their realization in the flesh and blood of the living human being. The human body is not a separate part of the human being; it *is* the human being, viewed from the aspect of his material presence in this world.

In ordinary language we accept this when we say, for instance, that we have hurt *ourselves* when we have hurt our head against a protruding beam or when a stone fell on our toes. The person who slaps me in the face or caresses my cheek touches *me*. The head, the toe, the cheek—all this is *I*. The reference to a specific part of the body indicates the place where *I* came in contact with the outside world in a specific manner. It not only indicates the place of contact, but is also one of the means which conveys the human quality of the contact to me. The slap in the face or caress of the cheek gives me a concrete awareness of the kind of feeling which is involved. It incorporates the angry or the loving relationship between me and the other person, while at the same time it expresses to some extent the depth of that feeling.

Thus, the bodily dimension immeasurably transcends the biochemical composition of the body. It is the animated or humanized physical existence of man. What the exact meaning is of this animation or humanization—or, if one prefers, this spiritualization of matter by the human spirit—has been the topic of study and research by philosophers, theologians and scientists for many decades. No satisfactory answer has been given yet, and it isn't likely that it will be given in the near future. Personally we are inclined to search in the direction indicated by Edward Schillebeeckx[10] and many others. In his approach he opposes strongly the idea of soul and body as two more or less independent units which are brought together in a specific manner that is external to their own way of being. We should rather see man's body as an *aspect of human subjectivity*—that is to say, the human being is man precisely insofar as he is material. Thus we accept that the spirit is not the body, and that the body cannot be identified with the spirit, but neither of them may be considered independently from the other.

The mutual interaction of the one upon the other has been noticed by all scientists. Ignace Lepp in *The Depths of the Soul* describes this in his own way. He says: "It is true that brain damage has direct repercussions on the most spiritual psychic activities. But it is equally true that bodily ills, such as tuberculosis and stomach ulcers, and probably also cancer, are often symptoms of psychic disorder." [11] But despite this mutual influence and mutual conditioning of the corporeal and spiritual aspects, there is always an element in the human action which cannot be reduced to corporeal conditioning. This is the element of free self-determination toward a specific action. The living organism in man is a source of energy and emanates forces. However, as James Somerville explains in *Total Commitment*,[12] although the voluntary action makes use of the resources of instinctive spontaneity, the determination to employ these forces in view of a chosen end is not identical with any one of them. In the self-determination a new and novel power is revealed which transcends everything that has prepared the way for it.

Every scientific study in the field of psychology and psychiatry irrefutably shows the extremely close interaction between corporeal and psychic aspects of the human being, while at the same time it is generally accepted that the one cannot be reduced to the other. But if we must accept this close interaction, then we must also accept that somehow the spiritual animates the living corporeal aspects. It does so, not by simply imposing itself upon the corporeal, but by expressing itself in the corporeal. The corporeal, being subject to biochemical laws, has an innate tendency to lead to a certain result while it retains an openness for more than one possible expression. This existing tendency has its influence upon the spiritual aspect of the human action, so that we can truly speak of a corporeal dimension in every human action.

An interesting and valuable effort to understand the influence of the corporeal upon the human action is made by Rollo May in his book *Love and Will*. We refer here specifically to Chapter Nine where the author speaks about "intentionality." Intentionality is first of all the purpose in the mind of the agent to be attentive to certain qualities. The middle-income person who needs a new car to commute from his house to the station every day will not be interested in a Rolls Royce. His goal will be an inexpensive but solid car. He will be very alert to these two aspects. Everything which lies beyond these aspects will hardly enter his conscious mind. We may call this "the subjective intentionality." But at the same time the objects outside him have the tendency to draw his attention to qualities for which he is looking. The objective and the material world has the tendency to display its own purpose and possibilities. We may call this "the objective intentionality."

The subjective intentionality is a certain need in the individual; it is the urge of preservation and development. This can be an unconscious process, as, for instance, in the biochemical structures. These ask for a certain form of support and sustainment. This urge for preservation and development has in the human being also a conscious aspect, which results from the unconscious demands of man's physical existence and the conscious requirements for self-development in a specific environment. The objective intentionality is the quality in the object which reveals the purpose for which it can be used. An apple may present itself as an edible object, but as a useless object for building material. A stone will most likely show the opposite qualities. Every existing creature offers itself in a certain form of usefulness and thus it appeals to the needs of other creatures. Whenever subjective intentionality and objective intentionality harmonize, it is likely that some form of action will follow. The mutual attraction brings them together. Reversely, it is also possible that the different intentionalities are mutually destructive. The union of the two objects would mean a threat or even the destruction of either one. So when water and fire come together, either the water will evaporate or the fire will be extinguished. Let us try to describe briefly what happens in the human being in terms of these tendencies.

The living biochemical structures in man tend to be completed-in-action in a certain form, or rather in a certain variety of possible forms of activation. One form is perhaps more predominant than the other. Physical conditions, past experiences and social pressures intensify and strengthen certain possibilities in the individual, so that he will develop a strong tendency toward a specific form of self-expression. This tendency toward a specific form of self-realization we may call "passion."

Passion is one of the most valuable aspects of the human reality. All the specific human qualities of self-determination, the ability to give an interpersonal response and the whole material depth of man fuse together into one human urge. Passion leads man to the full expression of the human totality. His action will then not be the cold intellectual and impersonal approach to the other, but the full warmth of human emotional capacities is activated and communicates itself to others. Man will then be able to convey his deep personal appreciation of the other, express a fully human respect and build up a deeply felt human inter-relationship.

Unfortunately, too often passion is identified with irrational emotional drives, particularly with sexual drives. That's why people were urged to "suppress" their passions and even their emotions and feelings in order not to be "carried away." As a result other persons were often treated as objects who had to be approached according to certain "rules." It is undoubtedly true that passions can be destructive. For example, a distorted development of love can lead to rape or sexual perversion. A distorted development of character incompatibility can lead to a murderous hatred. But this does not disqualify the goodness and the desirability of passions as concrete urges toward fully human actions.

It is obvious that the bodily dimension of the human task deeply pervades the moral perspective of every human action. This dimension is the concrete circumscription within which human self-determination takes shape. We purposely use the terms "bodily dimension" and "moral perspective" in order to avoid putting any qualifying name-tag of good or evil on the material reality of the human action as such. What this moral perspective means we can best show in a brief description of some of the major human passions. Traditionally, passions are studied (and very correctly so) in pairs of opposite tendencies, such as love and hate, hope and despair, audacity and fear. The opposites activate the same human tendencies but in opposite directions. For instance, in love we want to be one with the other person, sometimes even to the extent of mutual absorption; in hatred we tend to eliminate the presence of the other, sometimes even to the extent of complete extinction of the other. Both love and hatred are expressions of human beings in their search for self-preservation and self-development. Let us try to describe briefly what happens in these passions. It is beyond the scope of this work to give a long treatise on love. For this we may refer to other authors.[13]

Love is a most complex power in man which contains elements that seem paradoxical. Man recognizes that for his own development he needs to be supplemented by other human beings, not only for his physical and intellectual needs, but also for his emotional development. The integral human being has a need for other human beings. However, it is not merely the experience of one's own need which attracts one person to another. There is also the sensitivity for a similar need in the other person. Love is not only a matter of receiving from the other; it is also a matter of giving to the other. In the receiving the lover gives and in the giving he receives. If a person responds to the need which he feels in the other, then he contributes to making the other a better person. He gives to the other. But in doing so he also receives from the other. This communication of self to another person in a certain way expands his own personality, since the other becomes, as it were, part of it. One breaks through one's own isolation and separateness; one unites with another without losing one's own individual identity. On the contrary, one's own identity and the sense of one's own value are enhanced by it. Love is then in a very true sense a search for self-preservation and self-development in which a new dimension is added to the individual and because of which he becomes more fully himself. The person who truly loves recognizes himself as a value for himself and for others, but he also recognizes others as a value for themselves and for his own sake. The deeper the response to these values is, the more the persons who love grow into a one-ness, but in the same process they become more themselves.

This value-estimation is not an abstract concept, but it is based upon the concrete reality of the living human being. It includes the bodily as well as the spiritual aspect of man. Although this inclusiveness of the total human reality applies to the response to any human value, it is perhaps most evident in the love-relationship between man and woman. Their mutual attraction has a very clear basis in biological and biochemical structures. Bodily tensions build up and seek release and satisfaction. But the human being goes beyond the bodily urges and seeks a unification with the other person. The physiological aspects continue to play a role, but they will not be any longer the sole, or perhaps not even the predominant, factor in the mutual attraction and response. It is the person-in-this-bodily-expression who attracts and responds. In this mutual exchange of attraction and responses the personalities broaden and deepen, the personal values are strengthened and grow, and the unity between the persons is enhanced, while at the same time the individuals strengthen their own identity as persons. This is a form of love which we call "eros." Eros is not the search for sexual-biological satisfaction but for personal unity in which biological sexual aspects play a role. We may describe eros in Rollo May's words as "the bridge between being and becoming, and it binds fact and value together." [14] It is the seeking of knowledge about the other and of unity with the other.

There is nothing degrading in the concept of eros. St. Augustine considered eros as the power which drives man to God. If eros is a binding element between human beings in which deeply personal values are respected and enhanced, then it does indeed lead to the love of God. St. John says: "But as long as we love one another, God will live in us and his love will be complete in us" (1 Jn. 4:12). When human beings come together in love and when they seek in this love the relationship to God, their being together would be a true expression of *agape*. Agape is then human love to its fullness. It includes not only the perceptible human reality but also its imperceptible depth and the presence of God in human love.

When we describe love as a passion, we may never limit "passion" to blind and/or uncontrollable instinctual urges. On the contrary, it includes the human totality with all its individual qualities and perspectives as well as the interpersonal relationships and man's relationship to God. Whenever in the human expression the bodily aspect of man remains the predominant factor with the exclusion of man's spiritual perspective, or when the spiritual perspective is so exalted that the physical tendencies are suppressed instead of sublimated, then the passion itself becomes a sick and distorted reality. In the fullness of being-human the bodily and spiritual dimensions must permeate and activate each other.

Hate is the opposite of love. Here again the basis is the way the agent sees himself and the other. Instead of tending to fuse into a oneness with him, he experiences the other as a threat and therefore tends to keep him at a distance or, in extreme cases, to eliminate him completely. One's psychological background, past experiences and social conditions contribute greatly to the likes and dislikes of other individuals. Such likes and dislikes themselves are not the same as hatred, but they form the basis for an attitude in which the other is seen as a threat instead of an enhancing factor in one's life. When this threat becomes very serious, a true hatred can easily develop. One who from his youth has been dominated and downgraded will probably feel very insecure in his approach to life. Most likely he will dislike and oppose any approach to life which differs from his own. The lifelong experience of extreme poverty combined with instruction about the social injustice committed by the rich can easily produce the fanatic rebel. The bodily dimension of one's life and one's entire network of interpersonal relationships predispose to a certain form of human self-determination. Except in pathological cases this will not necessitate this or that particular form of self-expression, but it is obvious that the leeway left for the expression of self-determination can become very limited.

There is no need to enter into a detailed study of other passions, such as hope and despair. These refer to a confidence and reliance on one's self, one's capacities, on others and circumstances, and to the complete absence of such confidence and reliance. Audacity and fear are again two opposite expressions of the same human tendencies, the prudent confidence in one's own abilities and the anticipated or real experience of defeat and frustration. A detailed study of these human aspects would involve a complete study in psychology, which would go beyond the scope of this study.

The important matter is that we see how the bodily dimension of the human being is not an external additional factor with regard to the human action. It may not be considered as a non-essential circumstance which only increases or decreases the degree of personal guilt. The corporeal dimension is an essential co-constituent of the *human* characteristic of the action and *as such* it must enter into the evaluation of the action itself. This has far-reaching consequences for one's personal decisions of conscience as well as for one's judgment

about the sinfulness of individual actions. These problems
will be considered in more detail later. At present it is enough
to see how the human task of self-realization involves the
human being as a totality. This task is the search for one's
personal abilities in their relation to oneself and to the world
of which one is a part. The human totality includes as an
essential unity the corporeal and spiritual dimensions which
together constitute the one human person.

NOTES

1. Rollo May, *Love and Will* (W. W. Norton Co., New York,
   1969), pp. 202–222.
2. Erich Fromm, *Man for Himself. An Inquiry into the Psychology
   of Ethics* (Holt, Rinehart, Winston, New York, 1964), p. 246.
3. Michael Novak, *A Theology for Radical Politics* (Herder and
   Herder, New York, 1969), p. 28.
4. Albert Dondeyne, *Faith and the World* (Duquesne University
   Press, Pittsburgh, Pennsylvania, 1963), pp. 168–179. Here the
   author gives a brief but useful description of the nature and
   structures of human freedom.
5. William van der Marck, *Toward a Christian Ethic* (Newman
   Press, New York, 1967), pp. 45–47.
6. *Ibid.*, p. 49.
7. Cornelius van der Poel, "The Principle of Double Effect," in
   Absolutes in Moral Theology?, ed. Charles Curran (Corpus Books,
   Washington, D.C., 1968), pp. 186–210. Cf. especially pp. 189–
   194.
8. Cornelius van der Poel, *God's Love in Human Language. A
   Study of the Meaning of Marriage and Conjugal Responsibility*
   (Duquesne University Press, Pittsburgh, Pennsylvania, 1969), pp.
   75–96.
9. Erich Fromm: *op. cit.*, p. 29.
10. Edward Schillebeeckx, *Kerk en Wereld* (Theologische Peilingen,
    Nelissen Bilthoven, 1966), pp. 227–277.
11. Ignace Lepp, *The Depths of the Soul* (Doubleday, New York,
    1967), p. 32.
12. James Somerville, *Total Commitment*. Blondel's l'Action (Corpus
    Books, Washington, D.C., 1969), p. 115.
13. Among other worthwhile treatises we may mention: Ignace Lepp,
    The Psychology of Loving (Helicon, 1964); Erich Fromm, *The
    Art of Loving* (Bantam Books, 1963); and Rollo May, *Love and
    Will* (Norton, 1969).
14. Rollo May: *op. cit.*, p. 79.

IV
Values and Norms
in Human Self-Realization

Earlier (Chapter II, Part III) we have spoken about the task of human life. This task is properly to develop all human qualities and capacities. Man must become more "human" at every moment of his existence. The more he develops in a proper way his human qualities, the more he will be the living image of the creator. This "proper way" of human development may not be understood in the restricted sense of mere individual, physical or psychological qualities. The full meaning of human development always includes a constructive interpersonal dimension, and within the human totality it includes also the essential transcendental perspective of man. The purpose of man on earth can be considered from two different points of view. Every created being reveals by its very own way of existence certain qualities of the creator. They reveal these qualities of the creator precisely by being and developing according to the laws which are inherent to them. The same is true for man. But man's created capacities include that he is to a certain extent the source and master of his own activity and development. In this he points to the creator in a very special way. In man's very being there is something through which he transcends his own worldly or material existence. We call this the transcendent purpose of his being.

However, man's orientation toward his creator is not superimposed on his own being. On the contrary, it is precisely by developing his qualities himself as perfectly as possible that man accurately shows forth his likeness to his creator. In being himself as perfectly as possible, man gives concrete expression to both his own immanent purpose and his transcendent purpose. The integral human purpose, therefore, is concretely realized when man acts in a truly human way.

In Chapter III we have studied what it means to act in a truly human way; it is man's self-determination within his bodily existence in a constructive relationship with others. The human condition makes it obvious that human self-realization includes many aspects which go beyond the individual person himself; yet these aspects are so important that he can only attain true self-realization by seriously taking them into account. Hence there are certain values and norms which seem to come from outside the individual, but which nonetheless are an essential aspect of integral human self-expression.

With respect to norms and values for human self-realization we must avoid introducing two sets of norms, one coming from God and the other resulting from human nature. The norms and values which God has given man are expressed in man's nature precisely insofar as it is a *human* nature. Vatican Council II describes this as follows: "Far from thinking that works produced by man's own talents and energy are in opposition to God's power, and that the rational creature exists as a kind of rival to the creator, Christians are convinced that the triumphs of the human race are a sign of God's grace and the flowering of his own mysterious design" (*Pastoral Constitution on the Church in the Modern World*, n. 34). Human activity and progress itself is an unfolding of God's design.

Man must gradually discover the values which society should have in keeping with man's personal dignity. Man must formulate these values, put them to use and express them in laws. Man will discover the laws of God to the extent that he discovers the laws of the individual and society and the relationship between these two. Again Vatican Council II emphasizes this point: "The norm of human activity is this: that in accord with the divine plan and will, it harmonize with the genuine good of the human race, and that it allow men as individuals and as members of society to pursue their total vocation and fulfill it" (*Pastoral Constitution on the Church in the Modern World*, n. 35).

Three aspects, then, must be taken into account for the establishment of norms and values for human activity: (1) a constructive contribution to the good of mankind; (2) respect for the human being as a unique individual; (3) respect for him as a member of society. God's designs for man—the total purpose of man—are contained in the realization of these three aspects and their interrelationship. Still we often speak—very correctly—about divine laws and human laws. The exact meaning of these terms we will see later. First we must study another important point.

Historicity of Values and Norms

The two concepts "values" and "norms" go together under the same heading here, although values and norms are not the same. "Value" refers to the understanding of a certain good for an individual or society which is considered worthy of realization. "Norm" refers to the manner and the limits within which the concrete realization of the value is possible. For example, it is considered to be a value to dress decently and respectably, and there are certain ways and limits which must be taken into account if one wants to give a concrete expression to this value. There is an obvious interdependence between value and norm. The norm gives a description of the value, while the value imposes certain limits on the norm. To dress decently and respectably is a value at all times, but the understanding of what decent and respectable means was quite different during the Victorian era than it is today, and the norms for decent and respectable clothing vary accordingly.

This helps us to understand the term "historicity." It doesn't simply mean that values and norms exist at a certain period in history, but also (and primarily) that values and norms develop and change throughout history. Man himself is subject to constant development—his knowledge increases, his insights deepen, and the possibilities of life and self-expression widen. There is an almost continual social and cultural transformation which, as Vatican Council II says, "has its repercussions on man's religious life as well" (*Pastoral Constitution on the Church in the Modern World*, n. 4). Therefore, it is not at all surprising that certain attitudes and rules of conduct which were acceptable in the past are unacceptable today, and vice versa.

Historicity applies to moral judgments. F. D'Hoogh says: "In more recent years we have discovered that morality also has its history; that it is a product of human activity throughout the centuries. Morality is not only a science which teaches us how to live, but it is also a science which develops from life itself, based upon human experience in history. Morality has not yet reached its perfection because history is not yet complete and man continues to find new answers to the perennial questions which arise from his existence in this world together with others." [1]

We need not give here any elaborate examples of new answers developed throughout the centuries with regard to interhuman relationships. The development is evident, for instance, in the relationship between employer and employee.

In the early centuries of recorded human history we see primarily a master-slave relationship, which in the Old Testament was religiously sanctioned. We see this develop into serfdom during the Middle Ages. The laborers were "free" but exploited during following centuries. Presently we witness the strength of labor unions, which sometimes exercise an almost dictatorial power over the world of labor. All these stages are efforts to express the human appreciation of the laborers in forms judged acceptable at a specific period of history. In family life it is relatively easy to trace the development from the patriarchal system via the extended family in which related families joined together in one common task, to the smaller family unit which is prevalent in our time.

Many other examples could be given to show that certain forms of expressions and conduct which were acceptable and good at one time can be unacceptable and even morally wrong at another period of human history. One could claim that the basic underlying concept of human dignity is the real value which was expressed in all these different approaches, and this value as such has not changed. A value, however, can never be grasped *in itself* but only in man's appreciation. Verbally and in abstract terms, one may say that the value remained the same, but its concrete reality was differently understood in the various stages of history and it was expressed in different norms. Thus we see clearly the historicity of values and norms. Man not only lives in history, but he also makes history and, in a certain sense, he *is* history.

The fact that human values are subject to change and development has very important consequences for the understanding of the morality of human actions. One must be extremely careful in the application to the present time of laws and prohibitions which were promulgated in earlier centuries. Though they may be valid still, the chances are that specific laws and prohibitions described a specific understanding of a value which does not hold anymore today.

For instance, it is easy to say that contraceptive intercourse has always been considered as contrary to the laws of God. But St. Augustine's understanding of it was heavily influenced by Stoic philosophy and Manichaean theories about the evil of matter and marriage. Only childbearing justified marital intimacy. This understanding of human values does not hold today and his prohibition cannot simply be transferred to the present time. When during the Middle Ages contraceptive intercourse was considered morally wrong by theologians and was even equated with murder, their basic reason was that in their mind the male sperm contained the complete human being, which was killed because of contraceptive action. Biology has proven how mistaken their assumption was and has put the whole moral evaluation of this action in a totally new light. Their prohibition, therefore, cannot simply be transferred to our times.

In and through the norms of the past we must first of all try to discover which human value was expressed in them and how this value was understood at that period of history. Only then can we study how this same value is understood in our time and how it can be expressed in a meaningful way. Going back to the example of the relationship between husband and wife in marriage, we see in the whole human understanding, confirmed in Vatican Council II, a tendency to approach marriage from a personalistic point of view and not primarily as an institute for procreation or as a contractual arrangement. This development in understanding has necessarily a great influence upon the intramarital relationship and upon the morality of conjugal intimacy. We may refer the reader for greater detail to our previous study.[2]

In this developmental process of the understanding of marriage we see another important point. The present-day personalistic vision on marriage does not at all exclude procreation or contractual arrangements. Rather they are incorporated into it and given a deeper human meaning. The personalistic way of looking at man is a general tendency of humanity, one that has come forth from the development of human intelligence, human understanding, human culture and human needs. The past values have not disappeared but, because of a deeper and/or different understanding, they have a different impact upon the religious life of man. Such new developments in understanding may be called "the signs of the times."

Vatican Council II tried to define this expression "signs of the times." A subcommission proposed the following definition: "Signs of the times are phenomena or human evaluations which mark a certain period of history because of their frequent occurrence and general acceptance and because they express the needs and desires of contemporary humanity." [3] Vatican Council mentioned a few other evaluative developments in human understanding.

In the *Declaration on Religious Freedom* (n. 1) the Council states how "a sense of the dignity of the human person has been impressing itself more and more deeply on the consciousness of contemporary man." This has its consequences in the moral approach to life, because it triggers the increasing demand "that men should act on their own judgment, enjoying and making use of a responsible freedom." The greater personal responsibility gives a different perspective to human activity as well.

The *Pastoral Constitution on the Church in the Modern World* inculcates a deep respect for human labor because of the "autonomy of earthly affairs" (n. 36). By God's command, man is the master of creation, and "there is an increase in the number of men and women who are conscious that they themselves are the authors and the artisans of the culture in their community" (n. 55). The advances in technology and the communications media emphasize the social nature of man, since "every day human interdependence grows more tightly drawn and spreads by degrees over the whole world" (n. 26). This places special demands upon individuals and nations and makes selfish isolationism more evil. "Every social group must take account of the needs and legitimate aspirations of other groups, and even of the general welfare of the entire human family" (n. 26).

In these and many other signs of the times, man has the task to find the proper direction and expression of his life. The Pastoral Constitution describes this task as "to labor to decipher authentic signs of God's presence and purpose in the happenings, needs and desires" (n. 11) of humanity. Religious conviction and faith in Christ play an important role in this search. This role is not a superimposition, but a deepening of understanding and meaning by interpreting these signs of the times in the light of the Gospel.

This interpretation is not the development of abstract theories but an insight into the true human and earthly realities. J. González-Ruiz describes it in these words: "The Church does not create a world with its own separate values, nor does she offer to men an extra-territorial place of refuge for eternal salvation. . . ." The Church is not a kind of divine edition of civil society. St. Justine says: "The Church, just as divine grace, must penetrate men and things and thus sanctify everything." [4] This does not mean that the development of culture and progress in civilization is the same as the salvation of humanity and world, but the salvific action of Christ and the redemptive task of the Church take on a concrete shape in human culture and bring this culture to its full meaning. The whole developmental process of values and norms becomes integrated in the unfolding of God's presence in creation.

The formulation of values, then, is an effort to describe in human words the purpose of man's existence and the concrete form of God's self-manifestation. In the acceptance of

God's dynamic presence in this world and under the inspiration of the light of the Gospel, the development of culture expresses the continuous creative action of God and the human participation in this creative activity. Created reality, especially human reality, is then at the same time both the surrounding in which God expresses his will for humanity and the world in which man discovers God's will and carries it out to the ever-widening unfolding of his inner being.

Formulation of Values and Norms

Human self-realization may be described briefly as the development of the human potentials. In normal circumstances this development goes on all the time. This applies not only to the individual but also to humanity as a whole. Consequently, the values which are to be realized and the norms which describe how these values are best expressed in human life and society are never static, but are subject to constant change. If, therefore, morality is to be authentic and true, it must preserve openness to change.

This means that in the progress of human knowledge and technical ability new avenues are opened to the expression of human potential. Thus existing values receive a new dimension or entirely new values are created. In a negative sense we see this happen very clearly in the development of warfare. The man-to-man battle of earlier times can never form the basis for the moral evaluation of today's nuclear warfare, for the latter's impact upon man and society is totally different.

Accordingly, the guiding principles and the formulation of what is good or evil cannot be established once and forever, but are subject to the constant search of humanity. Vatican Council II indicates that the people of God must labor to decipher the authentic signs of God's presence and purpose in the happenings, needs and desires which they share with their fellow men. However, this does not eliminate the necessity to formulate values and norms or make laws. Human limitations demand such descriptions and formulations. In an article on God's commandments and the inner guidance of the Holy Spirit according to the Scriptures, Hulsbosch says: "Everyone who believes in a personal God and accepts him as the sovereign creator of man and world will be convinced, on the basis of this belief, that man cannot be a law unto himself. He will accept that he ought to behave according to the will of the creator on whom he is totally dependent." [5]

If we consider this matter carefully, however, then we see a kind of antinomy in man. On the one hand, he must be the source and master of his own activity; on the other hand, he is totally dependent on the creator. Viewed from two different viewpoints man *is* and *is not* a law unto himself. This antinomy is an essential aspect of the human condition, but it should not be misunderstood as a contradiction. In the previous chapter on human self-determination we have tried to indicate how modest and limited the human power of self-determination is. It is essentially conditioned by the interpersonal responsibility and by the bodily existence of man. These conditions imply values and point to norms for human self-realization. They influence human freedom and are a law unto man.

But precisely because of his power of self-determination, man is not blindly subject to biological laws or the demands of society. These laws and demands, in their turn, are essentially conditioned by human self-determination. Within this mutual conditioning man must search for the values of his life; he must search for the possibilities of self-expression which contribute to the good of his personal development in all its ramifications. In this search he can formulate the norms in which both aspects, his task of self-determination and his dependency, are *co-determinants*. He cannot claim an absolute or separate moral value either for his individual self-determination or for his interpersonal and bodily dimensions.

Speaking about Christian morality we may not overlook the importance of revelation. We do not claim that revelation has added specific aspects or conditions which do not essentially belong to the human reality as it in fact exists, but, for a believer, "only in the mystery of the incarnate Word does the mystery of man take on light," for "Christ the final Adam . . . fully reveals man to himself and makes his supreme calling clear" (*Pastoral Constitution on the Church in the Modern World*, n. 22). The search for values and norms, therefore, takes place within the human reality as we encounter it in this world, but this reality essentially has a transcendent aspect the full depth of which was revealed in God's self-manifestation in Christ.

Natural Law

There is a widespread reluctance to use the term "natural law." It reminds too much of biological and biochemical necessities which are (almost) completely beyond the control of man. To use the same term with regard to moral responsibilities sometimes creates the impression that man, precisely in his human qualities of self-determination, would be subject to these laws of physical nature. This would mean a denial of the specific *human* qualities and dignity. Seen from this point of view such reluctance is understandable, but one might wonder whether this approach is not too restricted. It is the task of human life to be the living "image of the creator." This task belongs to the nature of man and must be expressed in and through the physical nature. Every process of development, every interhuman relationship, every human career is somehow expressed in and subject to physical nature, but at the same time it transcends this physical perspective. When we use, then, the term "natural law," we go beyond the concept of physical laws into the total human reality.

Within the human reality there are a number of conditions which must be fulfilled in concrete human expression; otherwise man simply cannot be human in the proper sense of the term. These conditions impose necessary demands upon individual human beings and upon the human community. These demands, which are so deeply inherent to the nature of man, are usually called the "natural law." In a way this expression is unfortunate, because the term "law" nearly always connotes an external imposition. Thus, consciously or unconsciously, this law is usually seen as an independent entity which confronts man and which limits the acceptable possibilities of his self-realization.

But this is not what natural law means. It is not an independent entity which confronts man, but human reality itself with its essential ability of unfolding its capacities; however, this unfolding can take place only when certain conditions are fulfilled. Man's need for air and food and drink can hardly be called a law in the moral sense. They are essential conditions inherent in human life for its sustainment; nonetheless they impose demands on man which have moral implications. In a similar way human self-realization, precisely insofar as it is human, is subject to conditions which cannot be disregarded without harm for the human totality. These conditions impose demands upon man not as outside factors but as factors that are essentially inherent in man himself. If we call them "laws," it is because we have no better word for them.

We should carefully avoid divorcing these "laws" from the person. Since man is a corporeal-spiritual being, the conditions for his self-realization may never be one-sidedly formulated in terms of either the bodily or the spiritual dimensions of man. Both dimensions are co-constituent for the whole human being and they permeate each other completely. Together they form the dynamic reality of man which contains the purpose of human existence, and it is in this dynamic reality that this purpose must be discovered. Then we may describe natural law in the terms which Louis Monden uses in his book *Sin, Liberty and Law*.[6] There he describes natural law as a dynamic existing reality, an ordering of man toward his self-perfection and his self-realization, through all the concrete situations of his life and in intersubjective dialogue with his fellow man and God.

By calling natural law a "dynamic existing reality" we avoid any danger of conceiving this law in a static fashion. We place natural law in the realm of growth and development, just as human reality itself in its individual and interpersonal existence is in a continuous process of development. Natural law enters into human life itself. It is the dynamic power in man which not only moves him toward the realization of his potential, but which also takes into account the essential conditions surrounding man's proper self-expression in relation to others and to God.

The words "relation to others and to God" do not introduce another dichotomy, but serve only to indicate various aspects of the same human reality. Without speaking explicitly about natural law, Edward Schillebeeckx clearly describes the underlying structure of it when he writes in his book *God en Mens*: "Human life is a dialogue between God and man which is carried out in actions. In this dialogue it is as if the material world and history are placed by God between him and us as a translation of his inner speaking to us. This world and history are also the means in which and through which man's attention is explicitly drawn to this inner speaking of God, but simultaneously they are the environment in which man is able to respond to the commission which creation imposed upon him." [7]

It is the whole human reality which is seen as a task. Man must understand and evaluate his present situation in order to make a constructive contribution to the realization of the whole human existence. He must learn from the successes and failures of the past to discern which values and expressions are more essential and more constructive and then act accordingly. In a very true sense we may say that creation has been placed in the hands of man and has been entrusted to his decisions. If we can accept that God created man to his own image, then we can also see that he gave to man the power to contribute to the development of creation or to counteract it.

If we are not mistaken, this is also what St. Thomas Aquinas (*S.T.* I–II, 91, 2) tried to convey to his readers. He says that every creature exists because of God's eternal design. He calls this design "the eternal law." By the fact that God gave them existence, all creatures participate in this eternal law insofar as they have an inclination to perform acts which lead to their fulfillment. For man Aquinas accepts a special kind of participation, because man participates not only in existence but also in the divine providence—namely, insofar as *man is able to take care of himself and of others.* Aquinas calls this "a participation in the eternal design itself." In the language of St. Thomas this "eternal design"—the *ratio aeterna*—not only points to the plan which exists in God from all eternity, but includes the production of this design itself. Therefore, in a participated way man is by virtue of God's gift a co-producer-with-God of the design of creation. Then Thomas continues to say that "the light of natural reason which belongs to the natural law, and through which man understands what is good or evil, is nothing but an imprint of the divine light within us." When Thomas, then, describes the natural law as "a participation of the rational creature in the eternal law," he means much more than saying that man simply discovers biological or psychological laws which have to be followed.

Man has the task to shape his own existence and to direct his own life to become more deeply the living image of the creator by developing his own human existence. Only by doing this can he be himself. It is evident that this shaping of one's existence and this directing of one's own life have entirely different dimensions now than they had in Thomas' time, but this does not change the principle. With Schillebeeckx we can describe natural law as "the holy will of God insofar as this will manifests itself through our understanding of the objective values of created reality." [8]

One might complain that this approach takes away the absoluteness of the natural law. But precisely the opposite seems to be true to us. Natural law has the same absoluteness as human reality itself. In whatever stage of history or development man exists, it is always his absolute task to realize himself as the image of the creator. The way in which he expresses himself is relative to the stage of development which he had reached at a certain period of history. This same relativity communicates itself to natural law.

Earlier we have said that the human condition imposes certain demands upon man which he must fulfill if he wants to realize himself properly. These demands can be called the ethical imperatives which are necessary for a specific stage in history. They can and must be formulated and are indeed for that specific period the natural law. But a dynamic and developing existence can never be fully grasped and formulated once and forever. The very concept of dynamic development means that new situations will arise and that new aspects will be discovered. These may refine existing ethical demands, or they may make them entirely obsolete. Unfortunately formulated ethical imperatives have often been mistaken for unchangeable demands of natural law, while in reality they were only the understanding of natural law at a given moment of history.

History shows numerous examples of such development. In the Old Testament we see that polygamy was not uncommon even among "holy men." According to Christ himself, Moses allowed them to do so because of the hardness of their hearts. If Moses could allow them to do so, this can only mean that he formulated in concrete words the acceptable and constructive understanding of the man-woman relationship in marriage for his time. Again, today we consider it contrary to natural law to kill prisoners of war. But in the Old Testament God is represented as commanding Saul to do so. This, again, was the formulation of what was acceptable at that time. During the Middle Ages money had a different role and function than it has today. To take any form of interest on money was considered as usury and consequently a violation of natural law. When the meaning and function of money in human society changed, this ethical imperative eliminated itself.

These few examples may help us see that natural law and human reality coincide, but also that natural law can only be described in ethical imperatives valid for a particular period of history, and which change with subsequent human development. Let us add, however, that the more intimately an ethical imperative is connected with human existence itself, the slower its appreciation will change. For instance, our evaluation of "usury" changes much more easily than that of the value of human life.

Natural Law and Christianity

In Chapter II we explained that the coming of Christ did not mean an addition to an already existing human reality, but the full revelation of the depth-dimension of human life. Christ did not come to abolish any laws but to reveal their full meaning, "to bring them to perfection." Therefore, natural law was not abolished by Christ, nor did Christ bring some additions to it. In the coming and in the teaching of Christ, natural law remained what it was, but it received a new depth-dimension, so that in the fulfillment of this natural law the full human self-realization could take place. The teaching of Christ meant in a number of cases the reformulation of ethical imperatives.

One example of this we see in his statement on the indissolubility of marriage (Mt. 19:3–12). He points out that in the time of Moses the full meaning of indissolubility could not be understood and divorce was allowed under certain conditions. In the light of his message, the deepest meaning of marriage as the living expression of God's unreserved love for humanity and the human response to God could be understood. In this revelation the formulation of Moses was outdated and had to make room for a new formulation. Christ said this with the words: "In the beginning it was not so."

It is this teaching which Vatican Council II brings into focus when it explains in the *Pastoral Constitution on the Church in the Modern World* that human achievements "are a sign of God's grace and a flowering of his own mysterious design" (n. 34), and that "faith throws a new light on everything, manifests God's design for man's total vocation and thus directs the mind to solutions which are fully human" (n. 11). Therefore, Christian law is the same as "natural law viewed in the perspective of the revelation of Christ." We may say that the natural law is taken up into the Christian law, or that natural law is partially Christian. Both expressions can be understood correctly, provided we do not see the Christian law as an addition to, but as a depth-dimension of, natural law.

Natural Law and the Decalogue

In the past it was not uncommon, and perhaps it is not uncommon even today, to consider the decalogue as natural law. Earlier we have mentioned that natural law can be known only through its ethical imperatives. The more basic these imperatives are, the wider their validity and the more difficult it will be (or the longer it will take) to reformulate them. The decalogue is a list of such basic ethical imperatives. Reading in the Bible how the reception and promulgation of the decalogue took place, accompanied by astonishing natural phenomena, one is easily inclined to see here a direct issuance of laws by God himself and assume that such laws are given once and forever.

The decalogue occurs in the Bible in two different forms in Exodus 20:2–17 and Deuteronomy 5:6–21. The study of its exegesis, historical development, authorship and connection with other sources is beyond the scope of our study here. We accept here that it is the law of the covenant between Yahweh and the Israelite people. But this should not obscure the fact that the decalogue reflects the basic demands of man's self-realization in his relation to God, to himself and to his fellow man. These basic demands are expressed in terms which could be understood at that specific time of history. Their interpretation in the Old Testament was markedly different from the interpretation today. For concise and solid studies on these points, we may refer to McKenzie's *Dictionary of the Bible* and to Botterweck's article "The Form and Growth of the Decalogue." [9] For our purpose here it suffices to indicate a few brief points.

The introduction to the decalogue: "I am the Lord your God who brought you out of the land of Egypt, out of the house of slavery" (Ex. 20:1), places the whole covenant under the dependency of Yahweh. It directly goes counter to the multiplicity of gods which existed in surrounding nations and cultures. Hence the positive proscription of the use of the name of God and of images of God. In the surrounding cultures the name and image of the gods meant an identification of the god with a man-made object. In these terms, accessible to the understanding of the people of that time, the truth of God's transcendence was explained, and in the light of this the further human obligations could be understood.

There were demands for respect for human life and integrity as expressed in "Thou shalt not kill." This command, however, did not exclude the "lawful" killing of prisoners of war. It described in general terms the interhuman respect and relationships which prevailed at that time. The command "Thou shalt not commit adultery" referred directly to sexual relations with a woman who was the property of another man. Other extramarital relationships were not included in this commandment. The married man who had extramarital relations with an unmarried woman did not commit adultery. So the whole concept of adultery as expressed in the Bible is culture-bound.

All this does not minimize the value of the decalogue, but it makes us realize that the decalogue speaks the language and reflects the understanding of a specific period in human history. The understanding and the insights of that specific period were the contemporary expression of the human relationship with God. Thus the decalogue is not the same as natural law, but rather the formulation of the most essential human values. These human values retain the same validity today; they express the transcendent vocation of man which he must live in his interhuman relationship. The formulation of the decalogue also remains valid, but its interpretation must differ widely from the interpretation given to it at the time of its origin. J. Ghoos points out that it is our task to see in the decalogue its positive content, that is, the basic demands of human existence and human self-realization which we must try to <u>understand in our own time and conditions</u>.[10] Thus the decalogue does not constitute an absolute minimum of humanity which is to be achieved, but the basis for a dynamic approach to the fulfillment of the whole human task.

Human Formulation and Particular Application

We purposely did not open this section with the title "Positive Law," because we want to stress at once that there is an essential connection between the natural demand of human self-realization and its particular descriptions in what is usually called "positive law." The term "positive law" always refers to a particular command or prohibition given by a lawful authority for the sake of the common good. Frequently this is felt by the individual persons as an imposition or as an infringement upon their task of personal and responsible self-realization. Obeying a commandment or law is experienced by many people as fulfilling the will of somebody else.

An unavoidable result of this is that positive law is considered as something outside the person which does not really belong to him but from which he cannot conveniently escape. From a certain point of view this feeling is not entirely incorrect. Every positive law is by its very nature unsatisfactory; it has the tendency to place the value with which it is concerned in external actions, and it presents this particular way of acting as the best expression of that human value. Thus positive law has a tendency to present itself as something absolute. These disadvantages of the positive law are as unavoidable as they are understandable.

In earlier chapters we have stressed at various times the essential social aspect of every person. Every human being has the task of *self*-determination, but this self-determination can be accomplished only in connection with other persons. Not only do we depend on others for our birth and earliest education, but also in later life we cannot avoid being influenced by others and influencing them. This situation obviously creates a certain tension in every individual. The urge to self-preservation and self-development tends to override the development of others or to use others for one's own benefit. The essential task of self-determination creates in every man a tendency toward self-centeredness. In his book *Education and the Common Good*, Philip Phenix calls this tendency "the most important cause of confusion and conflict in the moral enterprise." [11]

It is precisely because of this tendency toward self-centeredness that it is necessary to outline a mode of behavior which, at the same time, protects the right and the ability of self-determination in the individual and promotes the good of the human community. This outline must be a formulation of the deeper human values which are present in each individual. It relates to values which concern the individual as well as his relation to the society. In many instances man must be protected against himself. Hence we find, for instance, a law against attempted suicide and self-mutilations. But also the regulations which seem to bear directly upon the society as such are at the same time a self-protection for the individual. A clear example of this we may see in the rule to stop for a red traffic light. It aims to guarantee the safety of the individual motorist as well as of the others.

Such positive laws formulate a human value in its particular application to a given situation. Thus positive laws are not necessarily a meaningless limitation of human freedom. Rather they enhance the human possibility for meaningful self-determination. We may say with G. de Brie that "a positive law is nothing but an imperative formulation of demands which human values impose upon us." [12] Then, if we correctly consider the meaning of positive law we do not see them as an external imposition but as a description of our own self-determination in relation to others.

However, in this description there is always an element of arbitrariness. The human condition usually allows for a wide variety of possibilities which all can achieve the desired effect, but this desired effect can be obtained only when all adhere to the same manner of expression. For instance, safety in traffic can be obtained by right-hand traffic as well as by left-hand traffic provided all follow the same rule. Which method is to be followed in a certain country is the arbitrary decision of the legislator. To this extent it is an imposition upon human freedom and a limitation of man's self-expression. But because of the social aspect of man, this "arbitrary" decision is part of man's value-realization. To ignore this aspect would mean to endanger the human value itself.

Since this positive formulation of human values and its application to individual circumstances is only the description of one possibility among many others and is furthermore conditioned by time and culture, it is obvious that such formulations are subject to constant change. In many instances such change is absolutely demanded because a particular description often no longer reflects the deeper value which it intended to convey. Positive laws always have the tendency to draw attention away from the values underlying them and focus upon the formulation.

A clear example of this was the ecclesiastical law which forbade eating meat on Fridays. Its intention was to express that man should not consider material living and pleasure as the ultimate goal of his life, and to honor by this positive expression the day on which Christ died for humanity. At some period in human history this might have been adequately expressed by the abstention from meat. But it was certainly not expressed by replacing meat with a delicious fish dish. The focusing upon the formulation of the law and the strict adherence to this formulation which was seen as a specific religious (Catholic) expression could easily reduce this observance to a ridiculous and hypocritical performance. Long before this law was "changed" it had outlived itself, and someone who on Friday ate meat which he did not like was more in line with the observance of the value prescribed by the law than one who enjoyed his favored fish on Friday.

This example can draw our attention to two aspects in the observance of the positive law. First, the strong focus on the formulation of the law tends to reduce the law to something merely external. It makes the law an impersonal thing, so that moral evaluation can easily be based upon external performances. The same stress on the formulation itself also implies the danger that when a formulation is changed, people might easily think that the value pursued by the law has been abolished. This was unfortunately a widespread opinion when the law of Friday abstinence was reformulated. The same thing is likely to happen again in other matters unless we learn to grasp the deeper human value in the formulation.

This leads us to the second aspect. In the observance of the formulated law, the realization of the human value implied by it is far more important than the literal fulfillment of the formulation. Thus it can happen that the correct understanding of the intention of the law or of the legislator urges us to act differently than the wording of the law would suggest. We may call this the "virtue of *epikeia*," that is, the search of how one can best express in concrete actions the value which the law wants to protect or to promote. Thus *epikeia* is not a search for loopholes in the law, as it often was understood in the past. On the contrary, it expresses a deep respect for the law in its true and human value. By the proper use of *epikeia* the human action itself becomes richer and fuller and will have a beneficial influence upon the development of the individual and society. It is clear, however, that the use of *epikeia* has obvious dangers. It may open the way for self-centeredness and disregard for the law. However, this danger is not due to *epikeia* itself, but to human lack of insight and generosity.

In studying the formulation of human values in reference to their application to particular situations, we have not yet mentioned which authority is legitimately entitled to formulate such values for their particular application. Traditionally we have been taught that positive laws come forth from three sources, namely, from God, from the Church and from civil authorities. The term "divine positive law" offers a slight difficulty because the only code of divine law God "wrote" he placed into the essence of man when he created him. It is the absolute law of human self-realization. But how this self-realization is to be attained is left to the evolutional discovery of humanity itself. In this process of evolution and discovery divine revelation plays an important role. Christians consider the "reception of baptism" and the "celebration of the eucharist" as divine positive laws, and rightly so. But these also are specifications of qualities inherent to man. These specifications explain in detail how man's essential aspect of being the image of God is made manifest in human expressions. They are perceptible expressions of aspects which are in man by virtue of his creation and which have been made known in the revelation through Christ. In their general meaning they are contained in the human reality itself. We may say that divine positive law is the same as natural law. It is expressed in ethical imperatives which are formulated and reformulated in time and cultural development. The natural law usually indicates a deeply rooted and basic human value which is expressed in rather general terms so that its terminology remains valid even through successive stages of cultural development. Examples of this we see in the decalogue.

Ecclesiastical laws and civil laws are the application of the same human values to particular cases and circumstances. The respective legitimate authorities can formulate the expression of such values within the realm of their competence. But since the law does not originate with the legislator, but with the human value itself, the real authority is the human value in the perspective of interpersonal relationship in civil laws and in its transcendent relationship in the ecclesiastical laws. The gravity of the obligation which is attached to a law does not, therefore, depend on the will or on the decision of the legislator, but on the importance of the value which it describes in its particular application. The opinion of the legislator is undoubtedly an important aspect in this evaluation, but it is not the only or the ultimate norm.

New Testament Attitudes Toward Individual Values

The life and teachings of Christ are the most profound source for the study of the living expression of human values in their interhuman and God-related aspects. Christ brought the message of salvation in words and actions. In his life we see a surprising and seemingly contradictory attitude. On the one hand, he seemed to uphold the validity of the particular regulations when he said: "Do not imagine that I have come to abolish the law or the prophets. I have come not to abolish but to complete them. . . . The man who infringes even the least of these commandments and teaches others to do the same will be considered the least in the kingdom of heaven" (Mt. 5:17, 19). On the other hand, with a remarkable ease he brushes aside some important regulations concerning the observation of the sabbath. His reasoning was: "The sabbath was made for man, not man for the sabbath; so the Son of Man is master even of the sabbath" (Mk. 2:27–28). On other occasions he seems to be even more severe than the letter of the law suggests.

Christ's negative attitude toward the positive legislation expresses itself mainly in two general areas. He rejects the purely external and the hypocritical observance of the law. Christ's displeasure with the purely external observance of the law was evident when he said: "The things that come out of the mouth come from the heart, and it is these that make a man unclean" (Mt. 15:18). With these words he reacted against the Pharisees who made the external washing of the hands the norm for inner cleanliness. He chided them for making human regulations equal to the laws of God. Christ expressed this clearly when he said: "This people honors me only with lip-service, while their hearts are far from me. The worship they offer is worthless; the doctrines they teach are only human regulations" (Mt. 15:8–9). Christ objected to the adherence to the letter while disregarding the deeper values which the law tried to describe.

But much more severely he condemned the tendency to use an external display of holiness and religious dedication as a means to be honored and praised. He made this very clear when he said: "And when you pray do not imitate the hypocrites: they love to say their prayers standing up in the synagogues and at the street corners for people to see them. I tell you solemnly, they have had their reward" (Mt. 6:5). He advises his followers to listen to their teachers, the scribes and the Pharisees, but to stay away from their hypocritical way of life. His verbal flagellation of the scribes and Pharisees culminated in the words: "You hypocrites! You who are like whitewashed tombs that look handsome on the outside, but inside are full of dead men's bones and every kind of corruption. In the same way you appear to people from the outside like good and honest men, but inside you are full of hypocrisy and lawlessness" (Mt. 23:27–28).

The true meaning of Christ's condemnation of this external and hypocritical performance becomes clear only in the light of his positive message. He himself was the personal and visible presence of God with man. He was the full revelation of the deepest meaning of human existence, namely, human self-realization as a task in this world through which God's personal greatness is visibly expressed in created reality. Human life should go far beyond an external performance; it should reflect the depth of God's presence of which he was the personal and explicit realization. Thus he could say: "If anyone declares himself for me in the presence of men, I will declare myself for him in the presence of my Father in heaven. But the one who disowns me in the presence of men, I will disown in the presence of my Father in heaven" (Mt. 10:32–33).

The whole human reality must become the expression of this transcendent perspective in human existence. The observance of the laws in an external performance can never achieve this. The imitation of the deepest values of Christ is an absolute requirement for perfection: "If you want to be perfect, go and sell what you own and give the money to the poor. . . . Then come, and follow me" (Mt. 19:21). It is only when man is able to see beyond the self-centered material security of human life that true perfection is possible. A merely external observance or a religious mask is of no avail.

In this light we can see what Christ meant when he said that he came to "complete the laws" and interpreted them more strictly than the letter would suggest. Christ went to the core of the meaning of the law. That's why he told the people: "You have learned how it was said you must love your neighbor and hate your enemy. But I say this to you: love your enemies and pray for those who persecute you" (Mt. 5:43). It is the constructive interhuman relationship, which is the living reality of God's presence with men. He also gave the same depth to other commandments such as: "You shall not commit adultery." Its meaning goes far beyond the physical action and respect for the property of another man. It includes the total human person with the proper respect for one's being-man or being-woman. Therefore, "if a man looks at a woman lustfully, he has already committed adultery with her in his heart" (Mt. 5:28). So it becomes clear in the message of Christ that he did not come to bring a code of laws, but to bring life, that is, to make man personally responsible for being the living expression of God's presence with humanity.

St. Paul's attitude toward positive law seems to be no less contradictory. In Romans 7:6 he says: "But now we are rid of the law, freed by death from our imprisonment, free to serve in the new spiritual way and not in the old way of a written law." But a few verses later (Rom. 7:12) he states: "The law is sacred, and what it commands is sacred, just and good." In 1 Corinthians 15:56 Paul seems again to go in a totally different direction when he maintains that "sin gets its power from the law." One gets the impression, as Jean Giblet[13] says, that Paul himself seems to see a contradiction in the law itself. The law comes from God, yet it serves sin. To make a detailed study of this point goes beyond our scope here.[14]

For our purpose here it suffices to point out that St. Paul projects a negative attitude toward the written law whenever this written law is understood as a source of salvation. The law on its own merits has no power of salvation. The only source of salvation is Christ, not man himself or any human activity on its own merit. To consider the observance of the law in itself salvific would lead to a spirit of self-righteousness, and this would exclude the gratuitous gift of grace. On the other hand, the law explains to men the will of God and as such it is sacred, just and good. If properly understood and lived in its deeper meaning, the law is a help for men on their way to salvation. The promulgation of the law gave men not only a knowledge of God's will, but also an awareness of sin. In this sense the law gives power and strength to sin. However, the knowledge of what sinfulness is also opens to men the possibility of understanding his own needs and weaknesses. Through this knowledge man is guided to a greater reliance on the mercy of God. In St. Paul's view, the written law only has meaning in the perspective of salvation history, but never on its own account. A careful reading of St. Paul shows that he sees the law merely as a description of the deepest human values. It is the values that are important, not their formulation.

From the study of the New Testament we can only conclude that the letter kills, but the spirit gives life. The teachings of Christ and St. Paul warn us against a blind reliance on the letter of the law, but on the other hand they make us see also the importance of the law as a source of knowledge concerning God's will. In this formulation of values and in their application to particular circumstances man must learn to discern the ways of responsible self-realization which ultimately makes him the image of God.

NOTES

1. F. D'Hoogh, "Algemene Morele Waarden en Concrete Normen," in *Dynamische Perspectieven der Christelijke Moraal* (Lannoo, Tielt, 1966), p. 76.
2. Cornelius J. van der Poel, *God's Love in Human Language* (Duquesne University Press, Pittsburgh, Pa., 1969), especially pp. 18–33.
3. M.-D. Chenu, "De Tekenen des Tijds," in *De Kerk in de Wereld van deze Tijd* (Paul Brand, Hilversum, 1967), p. 62, footnote 4.
4. Quoted in Chenu, *op. cit.*, p. 71, footnote 10.
5. A. Hulsbosch, "Gods Geboden en de Innerlijke Leiding van de H. Geest volgens de Schrift," in *Tijdschrift voor Geestelijk Leven* (Sept./Oct., 1964), p. 441.
6. Louis Monden, *Sin, Liberty and Law* (Sheed and Ward, New York, 1965), p. 89.
7. Edward Schillebeeckx, *God en Mens (Theologische Peilingen II)* (H. Nelissen, Bilthoven, 1965), p. 187.
8. *Ibid.*, p. 192.
9. Gerhard Botterweck, "The Form and Growth of the Decalogue," in *Concilium*, Vol. V (Paulist Press, New York, 1965), pp. 58–79.
10. J. Ghoos, "Fundamentele Opdrachten en Geboden," in *Dyna-*

mische Perspectieven der Christelijke Moraal (Lannoo, Tielt, 1966), pp. 129–135.

11. Philip H. Phenix, *Education and the Common Good. A Moral Philosophy of the Curriculum* (Harper and Row, New York, 1961), p. 6.

12. G. de Brie, "Integratie van de Positieve Wet in Morele en Religieuze Beleving," in *Tijdschrift voor Geestelijk Leven* (1963), p. 10.

13. Jean Giblet, *A Commentary on St. Paul's Epistle to the Romans* (American College, Louvain, 1967–1968), p. 193.

14. For brief though worthwhile studies on this subject we may refer to Joseph Fitzmeyer, "St. Paul and the Law," in *The Jurist* (1967), pp. 18–36, and G. de Brie, "De Bijbelse Radicalisering van de Wet," in *Tijdschrift voor Theologie* (1963), pp. 152–162.

V

Personal Conscience:
The Ultimate Norm for
Human Responsibility

With all due respect for the importance of objective values and norms and their concrete formulation in human society, in the final analysis it is the personal conscience which is ultimately decisive in the judgment about the morality of a human action. According to Vatican Council II, "God has willed that man remain under the control of his own decisions." However correct a description of values and norms may be, it will always be something external to man until he incorporates this value into his own self-realization with regard to his relationship toward God and his fellow man. It is here that we enter into the realm of the human conscience. "Conscience," says Vatican Council II in the *Pastoral Constitution on the Church in the Modern World*, n. 16, "is the most secret core and sanctuary of man. There he is alone with God whose voice echoes in his depth."

This "core of man's being" escapes accurate human description. It is the center of human reality in which the individual's potential and limitations, his hopes and his fears, his desires for self-preservation and concern for others, his physical dependency and his transcendent urge fuse together into one unity. In this core of his being, man truly "becomes himself" and will be able to respond to the creator, who continuously communicates to him his "being in this specific way." Here man determines himself either positively or negatively by fulfilling what he knows to be his vocation or by refusing to use his own potential constructively. This self-determination goes immeasurably beyond external descriptions of human values and touches the very heart of one's personality. The human response-ability with regard to his own needs and those of others is now experienced as a responsibility which must be activated in an honest responsiveness. Only in this dynamic unfolding does man become himself. Therefore, nowhere is man more human than in the depth of his conscience; but nowhere also can man know himself more deeply as the image of the creator, or can he forsake this image more completely.

Conscience: A Pulling into Opposite Directions

The word "conscience" tries to catch in one expression two aspects of the human reality which seem polarities. Philip Delhaye says in *The Christian Conscience*:[1] "On the one hand conscience is God's voice, this intimate presence of the Savior which leads the soul to a better moral life and disencumbers it of its weaknesses. . . . But in another respect conscience represents man, for he can use well or not the moral light and fortitude that are in him." Conscience is the strange contrast of experiencing at the same time both a freedom and an obligation with respect to the same human action. One has the insight that the performance of a certain action is a "good" thing for the concrete and correct fulfillment of one's goal and purpose in life. It is then felt that to do this is an "obligation" or a "must" if one wants to be oneself and that it is necessary to avoid the opposite action; but at the same time one knows that one is able to act either way.

However, the action contrary to the "obligation" is understood as the opposite of true fulfillment. The good that one understands is a force that impels toward action, yet it leaves the person free. The two poles present themselves as antimonies in the human person. Man feels that he has control over his own decision, yet the fulfillment of the good would be experienced as being in accord with his human dignity, while the refusal to act correctly would be felt as a downgrading of one's inner self, even if material gain would be obtained in doing so.

There are other seeming contradictions in the human conscience. On the one hand, the agent feels that he makes an autonomous decision. This means that the decision comes forth from his own inner resources. On the other hand, he knows also that his decision is greatly influenced by circumstances which are partly or totally beyond his control. This is experienced as a law which is imposed upon him from the outside. This imposition from the outside creates a feeling of resistance in the agent, who does not like to be pressed into some activity; however, this outside influence is so intimately interwoven with his personal self-realization that he cannot avoid it. He both likes and dislikes a certain action. He feels the autonomy and the heteronomy simultaneously.

It can become even more complicated when man realizes that many demands of his conscience present themselves to him as holy and absolute. He would feel most unhappy and unfulfilled if he would not follow these demands. But at the same time he may see how the same circumstances seem to make completely different demands on other persons. One person may consider it as a very serious obligation to participate in community activities that promote social justice and racial equality. He may feel that he would violate his conscience if he did not dedicate as much time to this cause as he reasonably could. Other persons, who to all appearances have as much free time, talent and opportunity to contribute to this cause, seem not to give it a thought and are not bothered by the issue. This is shocking to the absoluteness which the demands have on him. Still more confusing is that in the course of his own development his ideas may change, so that the absoluteness of conscience turns out to be very relative and accidental. One feeling of absolute demand disappears only to make room for another absolute demand. Each of these demands is the product of changes in human experience and growth of insight.

Another antinomy in human conscience is the fact that conscience gives its verdict about a specific human action, but in this one concrete action it views the whole human personality in its fundamental drives and in its particular expressions. The past, the present and the future seem to merge into a oneness. The background which led to this decision, the circumstances which gave it this specific form, and the impact it will have on the future, intellectual knowledge and emotional attitudes fuse into one reality which finds its concrete expression in one specific action. The friendly greeting or the curse, the caressing gesture or the hostile punch, include the human totality in their individual expression. Often one experiences an almost instinctive grasping of the whole personal value in a single action. Intellectually one might reason (or rationalize) about the greater or lesser importance of this action, but very often this does not satisfy the complete personal feeling. It is the appreciation not so much of what the person *knows*, but of *what he is*.

Conscience presents itself as a complex reality which in many points seems to be contradictory in its nature. It obliges, yet it does not interfere with human self-determination; it is an autonomous faculty which acts on its own inner resources, yet it knows itself to be highly dependent on other influences;

it presents itself as sacred and absolute, yet it is subject to constant changes; it directs itself toward an individual action, yet it encompasses the whole human being.

Despite, or perhaps because of, these seeming contradictions, conscience is the ultimate judge about the morality of the human action. In the human conscience man's totality is reflected. In his conscience man is placed face to face with two dimensions of his being: the immanent goal of his human self-realization in this world, and his transcendent destiny to be the living image of the creator.

Conscience in the Scriptures

Since in conscience the two aspects of individual self-realization and the transcendent human destiny fuse into one, we find in human conscience the perspective of man's total existence. In the past the study of conscience heavily concentrated on the concept of "practical judgment about the morality of the human action." Although this approach is not entirely incorrect, it has the danger of overemphasizing the "judgmental" aspect of conscience, and may easily lead to a depersonalizing of the deepest personal experience in man. The emphasis on the practical judgment tends to place the values of life outside the human being in the external actions, and it tends to reduce conscience to a reasoning process. The study of the Scriptures on this point will help us to see conscience in the wider perspective of the total human relationship in its interpersonal and transcendent aspects.

1. *Conscience in the Old Testament.* The word "conscience" does not occur in the Old Testament, but the personal human responsibility before God and man was well known and had a great impact upon the life of the people. In an extensive study Philip Delhaye[2] describes how in the Old Testament this responsibility was experienced in the *heart* of

men and how it was guided by *wisdom and prudence*. The heart gives to men a witness to the moral values of their actions. So we read in 2 Samuel 24:10: "But afterward David's heart misgave him for having taken a census of the people. I have committed a grave sin, David said to Yahweh. But now, Yahweh, I beg you to forgive your servant for his fault. I have been very foolish." This testimony of the heart does not merely refer to an individual action; it includes the memory of the past and thus reveals the human attitude, as is said in Ecclesiastes 7:22: "Your own heart knows how often you have reviled others," and in Jeremiah 17:1: "The sin of Judah is written . . . on the tablet of their heart . . . as evidence against them."

But the heart was not only a source of reproach for failure; it was also a witness to the uprightness before God, as we see in Job's answer to those who accused him of being sinful: "My heart does not reproach me" (Job 27:6). Through the prophets Yahweh made it known to the Israelites that his ultimate judgment would be based on what is in the heart of man, as we read in Jeremiah 17:10, 11:20, 20:12: "I, Yahweh, search to the heart, I probe the loins to give each man what his conduct and his actions deserve." Within this same human heart Yahweh communicates to men the law of his covenant, as he said through Jeremiah 31:33: "Deep within them I will plant my law, writing it on their hearts." More is involved here than cold intellectual knowledge. As Ezekiel 11:20 says: "I will remove the heart of stone from their bodies and give them a heart of flesh instead, so that they will keep my laws and put them into practice. Then they shall be my people and I will be their God."

The whole human reality is involved. The heart is the center of man's being in which he recognizes the law of God which calls him to the fulfillment of his human responsibilities. Man must walk in the "ways of his heart" (Eccl. 11:9). The heart, then, is seen as the source of human actions.

It gives witness to human deviations and to human goodness. But in his heart man also creates his own attitude toward life and in his heart he is personally responsible for what he is going to be. Thus the psalmist warns: "If only you would listen to him today, 'Do not harden your heart as at Meribah'" (Ps. 95:8).

This warning obviously contains the need for man's own cooperation, his willingness to continue a search for truth and to maintain a personal openness for what is good. Later in the New Testament we see how Christ condemned severely in the Pharisees precisely this lack of openness and cooperation. If the defection from the ways of God is a matter of the whole human person centered in the heart of man, then also the conversion to God is only possible through a true *metanoia*, a conversion of the heart, as again the psalmist says: "My sacrifice is this broken spirit; you will not scorn this crushed and broken heart" (Ps. 51:17).

If we study the concepts of wisdom and prudence in the Old Testament, we see still more clearly the degree of personal human responsibility which was involved. Prudence is understood as a human quality which leads to successful actions. It implies common sense (Sir. 38:4), or a penetrating mind which knows how to cope with difficult situations (Dan. 5:12), or professional skill (Prov. 24:6). But it is also a very important factor in man's relationship with God. King Solomon asked Yahweh: "Give your servant a heart to understand how to discern between good and evil, for who could govern this people of yours that is so great?" (1 Kgs. 3:9). The request of Solomon was pleasing to Yahweh and was of a totally different content than the knowledge of worldly matters about which the prophet Baruch speaks (Bar. 3:20). Although he speaks about human success, he also brands Israel's behavior as a lack of true knowledge.

Prudence includes the whole human being with all his qualities. It refers to knowledge as in Proverbs 15:14: "The heart of a discerning man makes knowledge its search, the mouth of fools feeds on folly." But this knowledge has its repercussion on the human conduct: "To a man of discretion, wisdom means a watch on his own conduct." Prudence is the attitude which guides man to an actual expression of love and respect for his neighbor, since "the virtuous man is concerned for the rights of the poor, the wicked knows no such concern" (Prov. 29:7). This wisdom which is so deeply interwoven with human attitudes is found in its fullness in Yahweh alone, but he communicates it to men as a gift and a safeguard (Prov. 3:19–26). However, man may not resort to passivity but must seek it with docility and experience: "My son, if you take my words to heart, if you set store by my commandments, tuning your ear to wisdom and applying your heart to truth . . . you will then understand what the fear of Yahweh is, and discover the knowledge of God" (Prov. 2:1–5).

Accordingly the Old Testament concept of moral goodness and evil shows the most intimate unity of these two human aspects of self-realization in daily human life and its transcendent perspective. It is the involvement of the whole human reality of intellectual, volitional and emotional qualities by which man makes his own life a response to God's calling.

2. *Conscience in the New Testament.* In the Gospels and in most other writings of the New Testament the word "conscience" occurs only occasionally, but its meaning shines through in many places. The mission of Christ was to restore the human relationship with God, and therefore conscience must have taken a central position in his teaching. In Christ's approach to the man-God relationship we find many similarities with the Old Testament. Often he speaks about prudence as a necessary requirement to enter into the kingdom of heaven. For instance, he praised the unfaithful steward because of his prudence, and he commented that "the children

of this world are more astute in dealing with their own kind than the children of light" (Lk. 16:8). It sounds as a reproach by Christ that too many people fail to use their human resources in the search for the kingdom of God. He advises his disciples to "be cunning as serpents and yet as harmless as doves" (Mt. 10:16). In the teaching of Christ the proper use of the common human abilities is of the utmost importance for salvation.

In the parable of the ten bridesmaids (Mt. 25:1-13) he speaks about the ways to enter into the kingdom of heaven. The five unwise bridesmaids were barred from entering the wedding feast because they failed to use sufficient human foresight in their preparations. And in the parable of the talents which the Lord gave to his servants before going on a journey (Mt. 25:14-30) it becomes clear that it is not sufficient to receive the gifts of the master; one has to work with them with all human abilities. It is, again, human prudence which is of essential importance for man if he wants to be acceptable before God.

All this, however, does not reduce moral goodness to the level of mere human prudence. Within the human activity reliance upon God and an acceptance of dependency on him remain essential. As Christ said: "Keep this carefully in mind: you are not to prepare your defense, because I myself shall give you an eloquence and a wisdom that none of your opponents will be able to resist or contradict" (Lk. 21:15). Human prudence is not eliminated here, but even less may the openness of man's transcendent vocation be excluded.

St. Paul says that "the terms of philosophy" are insufficient to express the crucifixion of Christ, and that "God's foolishness is wiser than human wisdom" (1 Cor. 1:17, 25). But in no way does he downgrade the need for human prudence. He wants this prudence to be inspired by an openness to God. He exhorts his readers: "Do not model yourselves on the behavior of the world around you, but let your behavior change, modeled by your new mind. This is the only way to discover the will of God and to know what is good, what it is that God wants, what is the perfect thing to do" (Rom. 12:2). Human knowledge and experience are of major importance for this task. Paul reminds his followers: "Never try to suppress the Spirit, or treat the gift of prophecy with contempt; think before you do anything—hold on to what is good, and avoid every form of evil" (1 Thes. 5:19–22). What Paul proposes is a prudent approach to human life in the light of the Gospel.

In the first letter to the Corinthians St. Paul deals with a problem of conscience. It is the first time that Paul uses the term "conscience" in the process of judging about good or evil. But here also the term includes much more than an intellectual insight. It may be good to treat this "case of conscience" in a little more detail.[3] The small Christian community of Corinth lived in the midst of pagan worshipers to whom they were often related by friendship and family ties. It is not surprising that difficulties arose about the eating of meat which had been sacrificed to pagan gods. When the sacrifice itself was finished, the remainder of the meat was used by the family either in the temple or at home, or it was sold on the market. This was a source of anxiety for some members of the Christian community. In their mind this meat had a special relation or reference to the idols because of the ceremony in which it was "blessed." To join in a meal with family and friends in which this meat was used, or even to buy it on the market for their own use, gave them the uncomfortable feeling that they were somehow giving tribute to the pagan gods.

Other members of the Christian community did not share this view. They felt very much at ease with this sacrificial meat, as long as they stayed away from active participation in the sacrifice itself. For them meat was meat whether sacrificed to idols or not. They knew that there is only one God, and they did not see any reason to stay away from celebrations with friends or family, or not to buy meat on the market. This free behavior of the "liberal" members of the community scandalized some, or made others, who were in their hearts convinced that it was wrong, follow their example. Although they ate the meat, they felt that their action was reproachable, and "their conscience, being weak," was "defiled by it" (1 Cor. 8:7). The problem was presented to St. Paul, and his answer presents some interesting insights.

He begins by stating that the material act of eating or not eating such meat has nothing to do with idol worship (1 Cor. 8:8). The important factor is whether or not one joins in the worship *as a person*. To know intellectually that there is only one God and that therefore idols have no religious meaning is apparently not sufficient. Some may know this intellectually, but they "have been so long used to idols that they eat this food as though it really had been sacrificed to the idols." Intellectual knowledge is different from total personal involvement. Their practical judgment is not an expression of the whole person. Paul appears to accept that one has to follow one's deeper personal insight. Therefore he says that "their conscience, being weak, is defiled by it." They are sinful, even if they know intellectually that they are not joining in idol worship. Although their conscience is erroneous, they must follow it.

But the "liberal" members have made a mistake also. They are right to think that their action is no idol worship and that they are free to eat this meat. However, in the use of their freedom they must take into account the whole community. Charity demands that they do not cause anxiety in others if they can help it. Therefore: "Be careful that you do not make use of this freedom in a way that proves a pitfall for the weak" (1 Cor. 8:9). If they are the cause of sin in their brothers, they would be sinning against Christ (1 Cor. 8:12).

One further aspect becomes evident in this case, namely,

that conscience is not a "post-factum" judgment. It judges the human action not in retrospect, but before the action is performed the agent knows whether the thing he is going to do is a correct thing or not. Based upon human prudence enlightened by the message of the Gospel, man must decide whether or not his proposed behavior is a constructive self-realization. For St. Paul all the aspects of the human self-realization enter into the decision. The laws of God, man's personal inner conviction, and respect for the conviction of others are all part of the human conscience.

Elsewhere in his writings Paul makes clear how essentially conscience is an aspect of the human being. In Romans 2:12–16 he speaks about the pagans who never heard of the law: "Yet they can point to the substance of the law engraved in their hearts—they can call a witness, that is, their own conscience—they have accusation and defense, that is, their own mental dialogue. . . ." For Paul the term "conscience" goes far beyond a practical judgment of human reason. It includes the whole person in all his ramifications. The light of Christ's message is an immeasurable help, but in the ultimate analysis it is the whole human being who in the individual and transcendent perspectives of his existence responds to the invitation of God.

Theological Reflections on Conscience

If our brief study on the meaning of conscience in the Scriptures has given us any insight, then the following theological reflections need not be very elaborate. Conscience is often referred to as a specific faculty in man through which he knows what is good or evil. But this experience of what is good or evil is concerned with the whole human reality rather than with a specific faculty. Furthermore, the experience of what is good or evil, or the knowledge about good or evil, is not a static reality, but it is inseparably connected with the dynamic development of man. Earlier we have said that human life is a dialogue between God and man which is carried out in actions. Our whole human reality and our human history convey to us the will of God insofar as they indicate to us how we must realize ourselves. Human situation and human history are at the same time God's speaking and man's response. The ability to discover God's will in this dialogue and to be able to enter personally into this dialogue in the core of our being is a special quality in man which we may call "conscience."

It is in his conscience that man understands that his interpersonal response-ability imposes on him a responsibility, because if this ability to respond is not used, man will never be himself, and he will be held guilty for not responding. It is the parable of the talents. To receive the talents and not put them to proper use is a cause of guilt and rejection. The responsibility which man experiences demands a responsiveness, a readiness to act. It is this whole combination of human ability, human insight, human experience, the acceptance of the transcendent aspect in one's life, which all fuse into one reality in which man knows that he must give an active response. We may say with Paul Anciaux[4] that through my conscience I become aware of the task of my life and I give myself wholeheartedly to this task. Or we may describe it as Gabriel Madinier does in *Man and His Conscience*: "Creation has been placed in the hands of man and has been entrusted to his decisions, since it is in the power of man to contribute to the development of creation or to counteract it."[5] This responsibility enters into his whole life, and there is no room for him to stay neutral.

Our theological reflections on conscience encompass the whole human task, and therefore they move along the same lines as the study on natural law. There is nothing new in this. Toward the end of the sixth century Gregory the Great wrote:

"By natural law man is forced to know whether his action is good or evil. . . . If he does not know that his actions are good, why, then, is he proud of some actions? And if he does not know that some actions are evil, why, then, does he try to hide these actions from others?" (*Moralia in Job* 27, 25; PL 76, 427, ABC). St. Gregory seems to accept this as a trait which is common to all men and he ascribes it to the fact that man is a rational being.

The same line of thought was taken up by St. Thomas Aquinas who distinguishes three stages in this process. He says that natural law gives to man the universal principles of law. Second, there is the habitual conscience, that is, the human faculty which is affected by these principles, and third, there is the actual conscience which is concerned with a specific action which evolves from a reasoning process built upon these principles (*In Sent.*, Lib. 2, Dist. 24, 2, 4). Here, again, the whole process unfolds within the task which man has received by creation itself.

In the study on natural law the specific human aspect of this task was described as a participation in divine providence itself. This task commissioned man to shape his own existence in the concrete situation in which he lives as a creature. Human reason certainly is the main factor in this process of self-determination, even to such an extent that Thomas could say: "Every decision of the will which is not in accord with the demands of reason, whether these demands be correct or erroneous, is always evil" (*S.T.* I–II, 19, 5).

However, this apparent supremacy of the intellect should not be taken out of the context of the whole human reality. It is the specific human aspect by which the whole human condition is elevated above the rest of creation, and in which the human expression becomes a participation in the divine providence. It is only in knowledge and to the extent of his knowledge that man can determine himself, but self-determination is more than a reasoning process. It is the core of the human being in which he comprehends himself as far as he can in the light of his destiny.

Vatican Council II points in this direction when it says that conscience is "the core and sanctuary of man, where he is alone with God whose voice echoes in his depth." Only in this total view can man, properly speaking, "labor to decipher authentic signs of God's presence and purpose in the happenings, needs and desires of humanity." Although some people call conscience a specific faculty in man, we should carefully keep in mind that this faculty comprehends the whole human being with all his abilities. It would be a mistake to reduce conscience to a mere judgment of the practical reason. A more detailed study of conscience in Vatican Council II may help to see what we mean.

Conscience in Vatican Council II

It was the specific aim of Vatican Council II to be a pastoral Council. Consequently, we cannot expect to find a theological treatise on conscience in its documents, but we can expect frequent references to conscience, since this is the heart of the man-God relationship. These references are spread all over the documents and decrees where they highlight how a specific aspect of the human task transcends the individual human reality and relates to the creator. This makes it impossible to arrange these references by a rigid classification, but it does not prevent bringing them together under a few very general headings.

Corresponding to a general view of man himself—the nature and dignity of man, human responsibility, and the human process of growth and development—Vatican Council II refers in general terms to (1) the dignity and nature of conscience, (2) its rights and its obligations, and (3) its formation and development. From the study of the Council documents it becomes once more evident that conscience is not an isolated functioning in man but that it is the whole human being in his total self-realization. No attempt will be made to give all the Council references to conscience.[6] We will make only a few selections to indicate how the Council saw the nature and function of conscience.

1. *The Nature and Dignity of Conscience.* In its study on the Church's role in the modern world the Council was deeply concerned with the message of the Gospel, but it states that "this Gospel . . . has a sacred reverence for the dignity of conscience and its freedom of choice" (*Pastoral Constitution on the Church in the Modern World*, n. 41). The reason for this sacred reverence is the transcendent aspect of the human task itself. In his own being man must discover the plan of the creator. Conscience, then, "is the most secret core and sanctuary of man. There he is alone with God, whose voice echoes in his depths" (*Pastoral Constitution on the Church in the Modern World*, n. 16). It is then also "through the mediation of his conscience that man perceives and acknowledges the imperatives of the divine law" (*Declaration on Religious Freedom*, n. 3). Therefore, conscience is for man the voice of God, even to such an extent that conscience can err "from invincible ignorance without losing its dignity" (*Pastoral Constitution on the Church in the Modern World*, n. 16), because "God calls men to serve him in spirit and truth; hence they are bound in conscience but they stand under no compulsion" (*Declaration on Religious Freedom*, n. 11).

The recognition of this transcendent aspect of his being in no way diminishes the human dignity. Rather the opposite is true, "for man has in his heart a law written by God: to obey it is the very dignity of man; according to it he will be judged" (*Pastoral Constitution on the Church in the Modern World*, n. 16). Human self-fulfillment and obedience to the voice of God in conscience complement each other, for as the

Pastoral Constitution says: "The root reason for human dignity lies in man's call to communion with God" (n. 19), and "Faith throws a new light on everything, manifests God's design for man's total vocation, and thus directs the mind to solutions which are fully human" (n. 11).

But the full human reality is by its nature an interpersonal relationship. Conscience performs a most important function in establishing a true unity among men. "In fidelity to conscience, Christians are joined to the rest of men in the search for truth" (*Pastoral Constitution on the Church in the Modern World*, n. 16). Where daily life in the world as members of the human society may sometimes seem little compatible with the responsibilities of the faith toward the Church, there again in "every temporal affair they must be guided by Christian conscience" (*Dogmatic Constitution on the Church*, n. 36).

Conscience is the ultimate source of human responsibility. Where errors because of ignorance or human limitations do not make conscience lose its dignity and do not place any guilt upon men, there the willful rejection of the dictates of conscience in order to dodge religious questions does not set man free from blame (*Pastoral Constitution on the Church in the Modern World*, n. 19). So it would appear that the nature and dignity of conscience as set forth in the Council documents stress the dignity of man himself. In his conscience he recognizes the transcendent aspect of his being which helps him to be more fully human and more intimately united with his fellow men, and in this full human self-realization, man's conscience will be the ultimate basis for the judgment of God.

2. *Rights and Obligations of Conscience.* Personal and responsible freedom is one of the major topics which emerge from the documents of Vatican Council II. It states how the Gospel message has a sacred reverence for the dignity of conscience and its freedom of choice. This can hardly be surpris-

ing in the light of the other Council statement that "God has willed that man remain under the control of his own decisions" (*Pastoral Constitution on the Church in the Modern World*, n. 17). This growing awareness of responsible freedom the Council considers "to be greatly in accord with truth and justice" (*Declaration on Religious Freedom*, n. 1). But if this personal and responsible freedom is a God-given right to the individual, then it is also a God-given task of the community to acknowledge and honor this right. Therefore, "man is not to be forced to act in a manner contrary to his conscience. Nor, on the other hand, is he to be restrained from acting in accordance with his conscience, especially in matters religious" (*Declaration on Religious Freedom*, n. 3).

This places a twofold task upon the community. First it must adhere to a proper moral code in the presentation via the social communications media, by which those who use these media "ought to follow such judgments according to the norms of an upright conscience" (*Decree on the Media of Social Communications*, n. 9). Second, "it will be the special task of the national offices (the press, film and radio) to see to it that the consciences of the faithful are properly instructed with respect to these media" (*Decree on the Media of Social Communications*, n. 21). This formation of a proper conscience has a special importance with regard to the education of youth (*Pastoral Constitution on the Church in the Modern World*, n. 31).

The individual himself shares in the task of the community. This means that his right to follow his own conscience may never jeopardize the proper development of the human community. Man does not exist by his own power nor for himself alone. "In the depths of his conscience, man detects a law which he does not impose upon himself, but which holds him to obedience" (*Pastoral Constitution on the Church in the Modern World*, n. 16). Increased awareness of the social nature of man gives every man a "growing consciousness of his personal responsibility" (*Declaration on Religious Freedom*, n. 15). The rights and obligations of conscience for the individual as well as for the society are completely interwoven. They belong to the total vision of the human reality, which is self-determination in interpersonal response-ability.

3. *Requirements for the Formation of Conscience.* The dynamic aspect of human existence makes it necessary to realize that a properly formed conscience is not handed over to man ready-made in a nicely wrapped package. It is a developmental process for which man himself is responsible. He must "labor to decipher authentic signs of God's presence and purpose in the happenings, needs and desires of human existence" (*Pastoral Constitution on the Church in the Modern World*, n. 11). This means that man must search for the truth in his own life and in society. The more he tries to keep the overall perspective of his life before his mind, the more he will turn aside from blind choice and strive to be guided by the objective norms of morality (*Pastoral Constitution on the Church in the Modern World*, n. 16). And while error because of invincible ignorance puts no blame on man, lack of interest in truth and adherence to sin cause man to be personally responsible for the de-formation of his conscience (*Pastoral Constitution on the Church in the Modern World*, n. 16).

In this search for truth man is not self-sufficient. His essentially social nature demands that he seek information outside his individual self. The deepest meaning of the transcendent value of his being is revealed in Christ and the Church, so that he must look to the Gospels and to the Church's teaching authority as the major source of information and guidance (*Declaration on Religious Freedom*, n. 14). But he must also search in the welfare of the temporal society and cultural values of his own environment and of the nations of the world, within which he must realize his human self-expression (*Pastoral Constitution on the Church in the Modern World*, nn. 50 and 87).

Theoretical knowledge, however, is not sufficient. Actual experience adds a depth-dimension to human knowledge which no study can supply. The practice of a moral life is, therefore, an absolute necessity for the formation of a right conscience. Only by living the human values can man fully appreciate the spiritual perspectives of his own culture and his cultural development (*Pastoral Constitution on the Church in the Modern World*, n. 31), and thus become truly educated in the moral values of his existence (*Pastoral Constitution on the Church in the Modern World*, n. 87). Vatican Council II does not offer a theology of conscience, but it does make conscience the central perspective of man's self-realization in his individual and transcendent decisions.

Obedience to Authority and Freedom of Conscience

If the free decision of personal conscience is the ultimate basis to judge the moral value of a human action, we may wonder what room is left for obedience to authority. In fact, freedom of conscience and obedience to authority are two concepts which too often seem to be on a head-on collision course. It would not be surprising if the reason for this collision course must be sought in a misunderstanding of both concepts, authority as well as freedom.

Authority is often understood as the power to impose certain regulations and ways of conduct upon a human community. This power is invested in one or more persons. However true this point may be, it is only a partial aspect of authority and in no way exhausts its full meaning. Authority is a necessity in any human community. Man discovers the necessity of authority in the human task of self-realization in which the individual stands in relation to the society. The necessity of the interhuman relationship expresses concretely that human development depends on powers which go beyond the individual's own being. But even the human community as such does not sufficiently explain the purpose of man's existence. Thus in and through the interhuman relationship man can find his relationship to God. God himself is beyond human perception, but for the believer his demands are made known in the needs of humanity in all its dimensions. In the human need for authority the dependence on God can be discovered, and vice versa, in the acceptance of God, man's relationship to God permeates his interhuman relations. The search for human values is a social as well as an individual task. Precisely in this interhuman search a center is necessary, not as the source of human values but as the center in which the many aspects and opinions focus and merge into a concrete expression.

Authority is not a body separated from or above the community, but it belongs to the community as a central organ of service for the discovery, the protection and the concrete realization of human values in the concrete circumstances of the community. The primary task of authority is not to impose values or regulations; rather its primary task is to be the central organism in the common *search* for human values. The formulation of values in the form of regulations and demands arises only as a result of the community's search for values. Authority in its proper sense is possible only in relation to free human beings. Its primary task is not to *impose* demands but to *propose* the formulation and expression of values which are living in the individuals in their own personal way and which need to be harmonized with the general good. Authority is the means to define the undefined possibilities of the human person.

In this perspective it is easy to see in which sense authority comes from God. God's plan for humanity is expressed in humanity itself. This plan is not contained in the individual

person as an isolated reality, but in the human community
which transcends the individual, yet which respects the values
of the individual. Since the one and only purpose of authority
must be the full self-realization of the individual persons in
the human community, authority becomes the concrete expression of God's will and presence with humanity. Whether
this presence and authority are best expressed in a democratic
or monarchic form can only be decided by cultural and
contemporary needs. It should be obvious that whenever the
persons or the organization in whom the authority is vested
begin to disregard the needs of the society, their authority no
longer comes from God. In such case it would be a self-as-
sumed and illegitimately exercised authority. Whether or not
such a situation exists will often be an extremely difficult question which an individual cannot decide for himself.

The same principles concerning the meaning of authority
which are valid for the human community can be applied also
to the Church. The primary task of the Church's teaching
authority is to announce the coming of God's kingdom of
love. The Church as a whole is the People of God in which
the Spirit of God is living and working. It is not insignificant
that, as Vatican Council I pointed out, the Pope personally
enjoys that specific infallibility which the divine redeemer
willed to bestow on his whole Church (Denz. 1839). But in
spiritual and doctrinal matters also it is the honest human
search of the community of believers which crystallizes in the
teaching authority. The teaching authority does not stand
apart from the community of the faithful; rather it constitutes
the heart or focus of this community; it must be the indispensable stronghold and guide confirming the expression of
God's self-revelation in human reality. Here also, however,
overemphasis on personal authority and personal infallibility
can lead to a display of authoritarianism with a suffocating
impact upon the movement of the Spirit in the community of
the faithful. That this has happened as a matter of fact can-

not be denied, but during and after Vatican Council II a slow recovery began to occur. The proper balance has not yet been found between authority and community at this time of history.

When authority is a commission to the community rather than to a few individuals, obedience too must be seen in a different perspective. Obedience does not simply mean to do what someone else tells us to do. Obedience is an integral part of the human task to search for the fullness of man's self-realization. It is the recognition by each individual of his dependence on and reverence for the good of the community. It does not mean an abdication of personal responsibility, but it is the search for the better expression of one's own possibilities in view of the human totality. The authority which demands an unquestioning submission of the individual persons oversteps its God-given task, as does the individual who wants to shift his own responsibility to the shoulders of people in authority.

Another factor in the collision course between obedience to authority and freedom of conscience is the misunderstanding of the term "freedom." Our study in Chapter II has shown sufficiently that there is a great difference between freedom and "doing what one wants." Genuine human freedom takes into account all the circumstances which the individual can foresee and which contribute to his overall development. The person who is suffering from a severe form of artereosclerosis knows that many kinds of food are out of bounds for him. He may like very much to eat these forbidden foods; he may, at this moment, have the opportunity to take them, but if he takes them he is not giving any proof of being a free man. Rather he proves that he is not capable of self-determination, but dominated by a biological urge for a certain kind of food. So also the boy and girl who go steady do not prove their freedom by having sexual intercourse. On the contrary, they prove that their value system in life is not yet integrated and that they are not self-determinant, but determined (or directed) by their physiological drives.

Freedom is the human self-determination in which interpersonal response-ability is actively expressed within the bodily dimensions of man's existence. This active expression of self-determination can be either constructive or destructive. If it is constructive it is a true determination toward becoming oneself. If it is destructive the action also comes forth from inner sources in the agent and in this respect it is a self-determination; however, it is a determination which impedes development and which makes the agent be less himself. As we have seen above, conscience refers to the demands which concrete reality places upon the person "to become himself."

Freedom of conscience, therefore, does not mean that one can do what one wants. It does not even mean that one can do what at this moment seems to be the most beneficial for oneself, since the well-being of others enters into the decision. But it does mean that a person who thinks in all sincerity that he *must* take a certain way of action if he wants to be truly and honestly himself has the right to follow this course of action. However, this always implies that he will see his action as constructive for the human community and that possible harm to others is reduced to the lowest possible degree. The person who acts in such a way does not act in a morally wrong way. Whether such a decision comes forth from a mentally well-balanced or imbalanced person makes no difference for the moral evaluation.

However, because of the individual nature of one's own personal judgment, it is possible that the community (represented by the authority) may feel obliged to prevent the action that the individual wants to perform. An example could be the conscientious objector against war. If he is truly objecting in conscience, the authority may not force him to take part in active war. But the individual himself must also respect the conviction of others who do think that they must participate in the war, and his conscientious objection becomes only actively constructive if he is willing to engage in some other activity for the sake of peace and human well-being.

Accordingly, obedience to authority and freedom of conscience, correctly understood, are two expressions of one and the same reality, namely, the search for the true human values within the human community. The difference is that they are considered from two different standpoints, namely, from the viewpoint of the community by the authority and from the individual viewpoint by the one who demands freedom. There will always be a certain tension between the two sides. Unfortunately, authority often does not understand its own task and becomes self-imposing rather than guiding, while the individual tends to overlook too easily the interpersonal aspect of his being. But granted the unavoidable and continuous tension, they need not necessarily be on a collision course.

Formation of Conscience

If conscience were simply an intellectual knowledge of what is good or evil, the formation of conscience would be relatively easy. But as we have said earlier, conscience is not so much the moral judgment of what man knows but rather of what man is. All the strings that weave the pattern of the personality, individual inclinations as well as interpersonal expectations, impart upon the person an understanding of what he thinks of himself, what others think of him and what he himself and others expect of him. Conscience is most intimately connected with the whole personality. We often see that people who are educated in the same social environment develop nonetheless a totally different approach to life, or that persons who grew up in the same family and whose life experience within the family and outside reveals no significant differences seem to have an entirely different appreciation of values. This difference manifests itself not only in their likes and dislikes and in their interpersonal relations, but also in their appreciation of moral values. In the same family one child may feel deeply guilty for the slightest transgression of parental authority, while another, educated in the same circumstances, disregards the parents' wishes without any qualms of conscience.

In such persons there is not only a very different personality structure but also a great difference in conscience. If the decision of conscience is the moral judgment about the whole human self-realization, then it is necessary that the development and the formation of conscience be on a par with the development and formation of the personality. To place the formation of conscience in its proper perspective, we must go back to Chapter II. There we studied the underlying principle of the human task, namely, that the capacity of self-determination places upon man a personal responsibility insofar as he is the source and the master of his own activity. Man acts from an inner source of action. Human action is the activation of the interpersonal response-ability, in which man is essentially related to others. But this activation can take place only within the bodily dimensions of human existence. All these aspects fuse together into the unity of the human action which is then either good or evil.

This experience of the action being good or evil is the domain of conscience. Conscience penetrates every aspect of the human action. But where the human self-realization is conditioned and limited, the quality of being good or evil is subject to the same conditions and limitations. Therefore the psychological and social conditions which influence men's self-determination and his possibilities of interpersonal response also enter into the quality of good or evil. The psychological and biological determinisms which influence the human action also influence its moral value. For example, the stealing done by a kleptomaniac obviously has a different human and moral value than the stealing involved in a carefully planned bank robbery. This does not mean that the psychological determinism can be simply identified with moral conscience. Ignace Lepp reminds us that "there is always an important difference between Christian morality and psychological morality: the former is interested only in the harmony that exists between behavior and conscience, whereas the latter stresses primarily the unconscious motivations of behavior." [7] Let us explain what "morality" is in psychological terms.

Studies in the field of normal and abnormal psychology show ever more clearly that much of human behavior is motivated by man's unconscious tendencies. The experiences of early childhood, the child's need for security, the urge to please the parents in order to avoid frustrations and punishment and to obtain gratification—these have left their marks on the mind and personality of the individual. Though the early do's and don't's have disappeared from the conscious mind, they have created an attitude which causes the person to experience a sense of contentment or guilt in the performance of certain actions. When such feelings arise, it often happens that the agent cannot pinpoint any conscious reason for these feelings, but nonetheless they seem to rock the core of his whole being. It is as if the earliest experiences, especially the parental approvals or disapprovals, have built into the person a certain concept or an ideal which forms the standard by which the goodness of every internal and external action is measured.

This "standard measure" is sometimes called the "ego-ideal" and is then considered a part of the larger psychic function which Freud calls the super-ego. It is the super-ego's task to examine every action for its conformity with the established ideal, and consequently the action is seen as good or evil. This functioning is largely an unconscious process that goes on continuously and causes the person to feel good or to feel guilty. If he feels good he receives the self-esteem and self-acceptance for which he is longing; if he feels guilty this self-acceptance is not only withheld, but he experiences himself as rejectable and bad. Often it is a vague and undetermined feeling, but with regard to individual actions it takes the form of a conscious ethical approval or disapproval. In psychological terms this is often called "conscience." Its task is not only to condemn past actions, but also to warn whether or not future actions should be performed.

Though this psychic function has a great resemblance with our understanding of conscience, it may not be equated with it unqualifiedly. The super-ego and ego-ideal are a residue of the child's earliest awareness of his total dependency on his parents and others. The child's helplessness did not leave him any other choice than to accommodate to others or to suffer frustration. The only way to be acceptable and to gain esteem was to submit to others. Thus the super-ego is to a large extent a superimposed parental authority which the person has internalized. This same authority keeps exercising its coercion even without physical presence. What has been communicated to the agent is the fear of punishment or the praise for conformity, but not the human value of the actions.

In many instances one can hardly claim that the agent is the source of his own activity; rather he is forced to an action. Madinier says that with regard to such demands the agent remains more "an object that is trained" than a "subject who is the source of value realization." [8] Only to the extent that the value realization comes forth from the *own* inner sources of the agent can we speak of conscience in the true meaning of the word. It is evident that this personal value estimation is most intimately related to the early human experiences. As we will try to show later, psychological determinism and moral conscience are not the same. However, at the present stage of psychological and theological development the ratio between these two cannot yet be defined.

We may, perhaps, gain more insight into the formation of conscience as the source of personal ethical value judgment if we try to follow the stages of the emergence of the personality. Jean Piaget says, "If we want to form men and women, nothing will fit us so well for the task as to study the laws that govern their formation." [9] Every human being has his own personality. He has his own psychic qualities which are characteristic of him and make him unique. In every human development an individual *self* emerges slowly; it makes the person aware of who he is and integrates this awareness into his personal life as a whole.

In the development of the human personality every stage of life has its own importance, but without any doubt the earliest stages are the most important ones, since it is then that the basic attitudes toward life are formed. These basic attitudes influence the individual's approach to and appreciation of himself and of others, and thus greatly influence his inclinations and his behavior. They necessarily play a major role in the individual's moral judgment concerning his activities in the future.[10]

Though intra-uterine life is undoubtedly very important for the formation of the future personality, an almost complete lack of reliable data makes it necessary to start with the moment of birth. This moment means an enormous change in the life of the infant. Its state of security, rest and constant gratification is forcibly interrupted. In a state of complete helplessness it is exposed to all sorts of stimuli which make it feel very uncomfortable, to say the least. It is in need of convenient forms of adaptation to the unfriendly outside world to which it is suddenly exposed. Only the loving care of the new surroundings can make up, to a certain extent, for the loss it suffered. If the reception in this world is truly warm and reassuring, the little infant will unconsciously experience that it is wanted. In favorable circumstances it can develop what Erikson calls *a basic trust*.

No matter how friendly and loving the reception may be, however, the infant will always experience certain frustrations, such as the discomforts of being washed and dressed, and the feeling of hunger. This creates necessarily *a basic mistrust* or an experience of hardship in which the infant must try to maintain its existence. The balance between the feeling of being accepted and the hardship which it suffers is of paramount importance for the development of the future approach to life and the interaction with the outside world. An overdose of frustration or an underdose of love creates a basic attitude of mistrust in humanity. Especially the quality of love which is given is of the highest importance. There is some inexplicable ability in the tiny infant which makes it discern whether the love it receives is a genuine giving or whether the infant itself is used primarily to satisfy the mother's desire to be loved. Somehow the infant seems to experience whether it is loved for its own sake or whether it must primarily satisfy the needs of the parents.

Approximately a decade ago an immigrant family with three children came to this country. The two older children went to school—first grade and kindergarten. The youngest was about three months old. The mother spoke only her native language, and in her loneliness she needed the child as much as the child needed her. Although the parents made every effort to educate the children in a balanced way, the youngest later had difficulties in being away from home, going to school, etc. One day the school psychologist asked the child: "If you could be an animal, which animal would you choose to be?" The answer came unhesitatingly: "I would like to be a porcupine; then I could put up my pins and no one could touch me." Evidently the child was tired of being needed by others. The unconscious needs of the mother had communicated itself to the child. It had been forced to give what it did not have. From its earliest age this child's world had been demanding, not giving. This basic experience influenced its later development.

This first phase of total dependence and of development of basic trust and mistrust flows gradually over into the next phase. Here the child starts to recognize itself as different from the rest of the world. It learns to crawl around, to stand on its own feet and to make its first steps. But these first steps, however hesitant they may be, are also the first steps into the child's "personally fulfilling its own desires." It has to learn to keep its hand off many things that are very attractive, to stay away from places which call for adventure, and to take care of his personal needs at special times and places determined by others. These first steps into autonomy, i.e., in going its own way, are often crossed by the opposition of others. The autonomy of the child in this stage can be wisely guided so that the child learns to adapt and to control itself without losing its self-esteem, or it can be made to become ashamed and doubtful of itself and develop a genuine dislike for others.

This period in the child's life will be decisive for "the ratio between love and hate, for that between cooperation and willfullness and for that between the freedom of self-expression and its suppression." [11] Nothing of all this is at this stage a process of intellectual reasoning. It is the formation of attitudes which nonetheless form the warp upon which the straight or crooked pattern of future behavior will be woven. It is the beginning of cooperation or stubborn opposition, the liking or disliking of others, respect for authority or an innate hatred for anyone in power. We only mention extremes; between them there is an infinitude of shades, and later life experience may correct many early mistakes, but the impact of this basic pattern may not be overlooked. During this period the child has discovered that it is a person in its own right. The next step will be the discovery of what kind of person it is going to be.

The third period is marked by imagination and initiative. The increased freedom of movement, the continued mastery of language, the wider experience in contact with his peers—all these contribute to the child's creation of a world in its own thoughts, adapted to its own wishes, needs and abilities. But here as well as in the previous period the outside world does not always agree with its enterprises. The youngster will meet with obstacles, which either come forth from his own inability or from clashes between his own wish-world and the adult reality outside him. If the adult world understands him and pilots him safely around the multiple cliffs, things will work out all right. It may also happen that the youngster is pushed down and overruled inconsiderately. Then serious guilt feelings can easily develop. Without a particular reasoning process and without knowing why, he will experience that his initiative is bad, but nonetheless he cannot resist the urge to follow his initiative whenever the opportunity presents itself. During this period of time the child discovers many things which it can do or cannot do, and in this process it learns also what it may do or may not do. However, for the child's personal attitudes and understanding it is of enormous importance whether this knowledge is given as a principle of guidance or in the form of complete rejection.

Although a certain knowledge of right and wrong has developed at this stage of life, we can hardly speak yet of a personal conscience. The youngster's understanding of right and wrong is almost entirely built upon the attitude of those who praise or punish him. The underlying interhuman values are not yet integrated in his personality. An action is good or bad according to the approval or disapproval of the adult world. Piaget's study gives many interesting examples of this attitude.[12] At this stage we certainly can speak of a certain type of morality, but the self-concept, the understanding of his abilities, of the surrounding world, and of the interaction of all these factors, is still so limited that one can hardly speak of a personal approach to life. True, this youngster acts in his own unique way, but he is still so dependent on the judgment of others that he himself can hardly be seen as the inner source of his activity in the sense of responsible self-determination.

On the other hand, we may see this period of life as the beginning of the formation of conscience in the strict sense of the word. The beginnings of self-determination are there, and the material with which the child has to work is precisely what he has developed during the first stages of his life. If he has had the opportunity to develop a feeling of personal value because he was accepted for his own sake when he was born, if he has been able to develop his autonomy and learn to adapt without losing his self-esteem, and finally if his initiative has been properly guided without imparting guilt feelings for the mistakes he made, then he will approach his self-determination with a high degree of confidence and with an open mind for his own needs and for the needs of others. But if these conditions were unfavorable, his respect for himself and his confidence in others will be distorted, and there are good chances that his approach to life will be very selfish. The understanding of God and the demands which God makes on man will also be seen, to a large extent, in the light of these earlier experiences. Then the laws of God and the Church can become valuable guidelines which help him to understand the values of his life. Or they may become restrictive and meaningless impositions which are to be feared, or which will be despised as soon as one can stand on one's own feet.

The formation of conscience is undoubtedly a personal matter for every individual. But however personal it may be, the surroundings play a major role in this formation. Where

the earlier stages of development are largely marked by in-
take and identification, during the later stages growth takes
place primarily through integration. The person (young and
older) tries to understand what he hears and sees, and he
tries to make this a part of his personal life either by integrating it into his way of life or by rejecting it. For instance,
the obligation of Sunday worship can become a respected
expression of community relationship to God, but it can also
become a burdensome and meaningless imposition on one's
freedom. In both cases a certain value has become part of the
personality.

The indispensable need of education becomes rather obvious. However, education is not indoctrination but the imparting of human values. These values will not be imparted
by merely being mentioned, but most of all by being lived
in the family. The personal life and honest convictions of
parents and educators have a much more formative influence
than their commands and theoretical explanations. The developing personality is always searching for the meaning of
his own life in his relationship to others, and he tries to express this relationship in his activities. It is the task of the
people around the child to present a meaning of life in its
total perspective. This means to present life in its material
reality with all the respect that it deserves, but its transcendent value should simultaneously be presented. The interpersonal responsibility should not be seen as a struggle of the
individual versus the rest of mankind, but rather as the human
community in which the individual must both give and receive in order to be himself.

In this brief review we recognize again the basic outline of
Vatican Council II which indicates for the formation of
conscience a search for truth and for information and the
honest effort of virtuous living. Thus far we have said very
little about religious instructions as a source for the formation of conscience. We need not say much about it here.

If religion is truly integrated in the life of the educator, specific religious instructions will do much good. If religious instruction is merely another "topic to be learned," totally separated from daily life, the chances are that religion will become a meaningless burden, and its impact upon the formation of conscience will be minimal.

Differentiation of Conscience

Since the formation of conscience is so closely related to the development of the personality, it is obvious that we will generally find in the attitudes of conscience the same differences that we see in personality structures. This differentiation does not mean that specific values are valid for one person but not for another. Rather it means that the same values are differently experienced and expressed by different persons. In this development not only the genetic qualities of the individual play a role but also the attitudes of the community. Everyone develops a certain type of self-appreciation which is based upon his insight into his own capacities and upon his success or failures in his interaction with society.

In this conscious or unconscious awareness the individual is continuously confronted with the society at large. This confrontation demands a continual evaluation or re-evaluation of his own attitudes and actions. Almost inevitably he asks himself whether his actions contribute to the betterment of the society in which he is living. Sometimes consciously, but often unconsciously, the behavior and the rules of the society influence his own judgments, while on the other hand his behavior influences the general trend of the society.

In the formation of conscience as well as in personality development, we should not see the individual and the society as two distinct entities. The individual belongs necessarily to society, and in his contact with others he has the opportunity to transcend his own individuality. On the other hand, society is made up of individuals who have more or less common goals. Therefore, society cannot simply impose its goals upon all individuals, nor can the individual simply disregard the good, the norms and the rules of the society. They are mutually complementary. As Gabriel Madinier says: "The conscience develops itself within the various communities. It is molded according to the norms and the ideals which it receives there and which it integrates increasingly. But on the other hand, the norms and ideals of the community do demand an effort of the conscience in order to be understood, to be developed and to be interpreted. This does not mean that the norms of the community are produced by the conscience, nor does it mean that the conscience originates from the norms of the community. Conscience and norms mutually interact." [13]

No formula can describe in what proportion the one influences the other. The early childhood experiences together with the experiences in later life certainly bear the imprint of the surroundings, but there is always the uniqueness of the individual which contributes something to each particular action and which escapes exact description and measurement. Every voluntary action makes use of the resources which the earlier formation and determinisms present, but the determination to employ these forces for a specific purpose is not identical with any or with the sum total of these forces. For instance, the person who from his early youth has experienced a harsh and rough treatment by others, especially by a certain social or cultural group, develops an almost spontaneous inclination to dislike every member of this group. There is a certain determinism to express this dislike in actions, but however strong this determinism may be, it does not necessarily lead toward such actions. The determination to employ these forces is not contained in the forces themselves.

Their application is something new which arises from the agent himself. In this new determination all the antecedent determinisms become means at the service of the agent. The action which arises has its origin in the agent himself. That the action occurs at all and the way in which it occurs is his responsibility, but in this both his personal predispositions and the circumstantial demands play a major role. When speaking about the bodily dimensions of the human action, we indicated that the circumstances are something not super-added to the human action but essentially belonging to it. They are the environment in which the self-determination takes place. However, since the bodily dimensions apply a certain pressure in a specific direction, the imputability of the agent will be in direct ratio to the intensity of their pressures.

Let us illustrate this with an example and compare two persons who get very angry with someone. The one becomes violent only after a period of constant provocation while the other becomes violent at the slightest—even imaginary—provocation. In both cases the action originates from the agent, and he is responsible for it. However, the circumstances because of which the violence erupted make it very likely that the action of the first one is less harmful to himself and to society than that of the second who became violent without any apparent reason. Both are responsible for their actions, but the action of the first is usually less "imputable" or has less guilt than the action of the second. We purposely say "is usually less imputable" in order to indicate that many other factors play a role in the imputability. Unfortunate circumstances during the early stages of personality development and bio-psychological predispositions may cause a person's anger to flare up without any serious provocation. Such reactions can be largely or totally beyond the person's control and cannot be considered as seriously "imputable." However, this does not mean that such a person can simply condone his anger tantrums and demand that others condone them also. In his personal conscience man must learn to grasp the ratio between his personal self-activation and his previous determinism, and thus know the responsibility and imputability which rests upon him.

Evidently it is impossible to classify the various expressions of conscience into well-delineated groups. Every classification will be inaccurate, and every form of expression of conscience will contain elements of other forms. Despite this difficulty we think it may be useful to outline two major tendencies or directions into which the formation of conscience usually develops. In this division we lean heavily on Erich Fromm's *Man for Himself*, where he speaks about the authoritarian and the humanistic conscience.[14] Following the same general division, we will first study the *authoritarian conscience*.

The Authoritarian Conscience

This conscience may be described as the approach to conduct and moral evaluation in which external authority, such as parents, society, Church or others, is merely internalized. This means that the standard of evaluation is not the human value in the total perspective of life, but the letter of the command and the expectations of the authority. There is little personal approach to life and decision-making. The explicit or implicit question for a person with an "authoritarian conscience" is not whether his action is good for his own development and for the community, but whether the authority commands this action. It is an effort on the part of the individual to dodge all responsibility. The only personal decision which the individual makes is to follow the will of the authority.

Consequently, although the agent performs the actions, his self-determination appears more like an extension of the authority than a personal self-activation. In analyzing this

attitude, we see many remainders of infantile stages of development. Often they are persons who never had the opportunity to follow their own initiative, who always had to do
what others imposed upon them, and for whom unquestioning
obedience was the only means of survival. In this attitude
toward life evil is not necessarily involved, especially when it
is lived in a patriarchal social structure; but as a rule it does
not contribute to the development of dynamic personalities.
With regard to conscience this authoritarianism can express
itself in a wide variety of ways and degrees. A few examples
may indicate what we mean. First, in extreme cases, it can
happen that the individual blindly follows the commands of
the authority without ever questioning whether the action is
good or evil. The fact that a command was given was sufficient. This happened in some concentration camps in Nazi
Germany during World War II. The individual camp leaders
justified their actions by appealing to their obedience to the
authorities. They disclaimed all personal responsibility, although they completely disregarded all respect for human
dignity, for the welfare of the society or for any other human
values. The only important value for them was to save their
own skin. One wonders how much cultural background, national needs, censored information, etc., had contributed to
create this attitude and how much this diminished their personal imputability. However, such a complete disregard for
human dignity can never be acceptable in our present world.
Such complete rejection of personal responsibility is also a
denial of one's own dignity as a person.

A totally different expression of authoritarian conscience
used to exist and perhaps still exists here and there in certain
people who seek perfection. With the sincere intention of
following the obedience of Christ, they submit in blind obedience to their religious superiors. They have a high sensitivity
to moral values and their deepest concern is to dedicate their
lives to the honor of God and to the welfare of humanity.

However, in their total dedication they included a total abdication of personal decision-making. Their action certainly has a very constructive element for humanity, but it is not always clear that this approach is a true response to the task of personal self-realization which the creator has given to all men.

It is not our intention to condemn what was so often considered a sign of perfection, but we should keep an open mind to the possibility that this blind obedience may have been valuable as an expression of perfection in a certain culture or in a certain period of history, while in other cultures or in other historical circumstances it would be valueless or even disastrous. It may also be true that some people need this kind of submissiveness because of their early formation, while for other, not less dedicated persons, it would mean the destruction of their personality. Our intention is not to criticize here, but to point to the authoritarian aspect of this approach, and to draw attention to the fact that blind obedience in itself is no perfection, and may even be a disease or a selfish escape from personal responsibility.

Again a different kind of authoritarian conscience is the scrupulous approach to life. Some persons are so overanxious to do the right thing that they are always afraid that they have done something wrong, and they feel terribly guilty about that. They need an exact outline for everything they do and the approval of an "authority figure" for all their actions. Their compulsive need for approval and reassurance and their unreasonable guilt feelings and anxieties betray the strong dependency need of people whose early personal initiative was broken rather than guided. They view failure as shameful and evil. Personal self-realization is alien to them; their norm is the real or imagined expectations of others. It is as if some form of authority is always looking over their shoulder, even when they are alone.

The degree of personal responsibility and imputability in

such persons is hard to determine. They experience their guilt as very real. There is, no doubt, a severe imbalance in their value appreciation, but to rectify this defect demands more than simply pointing out that there is no reason for anxiety. It requires a long process of re-education, which obviously goes beyond the scope of this work. All we want to point out here is the authoritarian aspects of such an attitude and the personality structure on which it is based.

Strange as it may sound, the authoritarian conscience manifests itself also in the lax conscience. This we see in persons who seem to display very little sensitivity to the observance of laws and rules, and who are very much inclined to do as they please. Concern for others is not their primary worry. The authoritarian aspect reveals itself in that they are their own authority. This means that it is not the depth perspective of interpersonal relations which guides them, but their own wishes. They usually have little concern for ethical demands or for the needs of the community. In many cases they plainly disregard authority and unconsciously assert their own total independence. They have never learned that adaptation to laws and rules does not necessarily endanger personal development and independence. They seem to feel that as long as no visible positive harm is done to others they are all right. No authority has the right to disturb their *own* authority.

Many other expressions of the authoritarian conscience are possible. We mentioned only a few of the more evident examples. And even in these there is an almost infinite range of degrees. The predispositions can be stronger or weaker or they can extend only to specific values. Except for certain pathological cases, the agent is responsible for the action which he performs, but the imputability of the action will vary with the degree of influence which the predispositions have upon him. These predispositions, personal and interpersonal, form the environment and the conditions in which self-determination can take place. They limit the extent in which the individual is truly the master and source of his own action. To this degree he will be morally responsible. This degree itself can never be calculated, but it would be a mistake to consider human actions as merely predetermined responses to uncontrollable impulses. This will only be the case in pathological situations.

The Humanistic Conscience

By "humanistic" we do not refer to a concept of man "as the ultimate end in himself," to the exclusion of man's relationship to God. On the contrary, what we intend to stress is "man in his total existence as a creature." This means that we want to see man as a reality endowed with an autonomous value which, however, in every aspect is totally dependent on the creator who communicates existence to him at every moment of his being. Therefore, the humanistic conscience refers to the proper functioning or disfunctioning of the total personality. It is not the response to a certain isolated relationship, such as external authority or imagined fear, but the response to the whole human reality in its individual and interpersonal perspectives as well as to its material and transcendent aspects. It takes into account its own individual abilities and capacities, but it is not limited by a myopic vision of self-preservation. It goes beyond its individual self into the transcendent and interpersonal perspectives of its being, without losing sight of its individual value. It is a self-realization in which the condition of the creature finds its fullest expression.

An example of humanistic conscience may be seen in the decisions concerning family planning as made by conscientious couples. Their line of conduct is not exclusively guided by rules formulated by ecclesiastical or civil authorities, nor by the urge for their personal gratification. Their whole human existence enters into their decision. The respect for each other as persons, the respect for the physical and psychological integrity in their mutual relationship, their responsibility as a couple for each other, for their children and toward the community, the meaning and purpose of marriage as the sacrament of love—all these various aspects fuse into a one-ness of the human totality. Within this human totality the couple see their relationship to God and the demands which this relationship makes upon them.

It is the depth of the human being in which man responds to himself and by the same token responds to God. The humanistic conscience is deeply sensitive to the needs of others, but in responding to these needs it is not guided by its own wish to do good. Rather it is guided by the needs of the other and is willing to abstain from action when helping the other would be experienced by him as an infringement on his freedom or dignity.

This may sound very idealistic and therefore unrealistic. It is unrealistic insofar as this humanistic conscience does not occur in its pure form, but it is always more or less interwoven with authoritarian traits. Humanistic conscience does not lead to disregard for laws or authority; rather it tries to see the proper meaning of authority as the crystallization of values and an indispensable source of guidance in human self-realization, without relinquishing one's personal responsibility. The humanistic conscience sees man as a dynamic reality always subject to growth and development. It is an approach to life which makes man constantly more human. It does not lead to sheer situation ethics, since its norm is not the momentary situation but the value which must be expressed in concrete human form. It does, however, lack the absolute security which blind adherence to law can provide, but this is no loss. Instead, it creates a dynamic and realistic self-concept in which accidental failure does not mean a loss of self-esteem. It gives confidence to man's creative abilities and makes man more the living image of the creator.

NOTES

1. Philip Delhaye, *The Christian Conscience* (Desclee, New York, 1968), p. 19.
2. *Ibid.*, pp. 51–66.
3. M. Moris, "Bijbel en Geweten," in *Tijdschrift voor Geestelijk Leven* (November 1968), pp. 631–648.
4. Paul Anciaux, "Het Geweten en de Morele Vorming," in *Dynamische Perspectieven der Christelijke Moraal* (Lannoo, 1966), p. 146.
5. Gabriel Madinier, *De Mens en Zijn Geweten* (Het Spectrum, Utrecht, 1964), p. 77.
6. For a more complete listing of references we may refer to A. Rabau, "Het Geweten en Vaticanum II," in *Tijdschrift voor Geestelijk Leven* (November 1968), pp. 649–664.
7. Ignace Lepp, *The Depths of the Soul* (Doubleday, Image Books, New York, 1967), p. 247.
8. Gabriel Madinier, *op. cit.*, p. 100.
9. Jean Piaget, *The Moral Judgment of the Child* (The Free Press, New York, 1965), p. 9.
10. In an effort to understand these early stages of development we lean heavily on Erik Erikson, *Identity and the Life Cycle* (International University Press, Inc., New York, 1959).
11. *Ibid.*, p. 68.
12. Jean Piaget, *op. cit.*, pp. 109ff.
13. Gabriel Madinier, *op. cit.*, p. 31.
14. Erich Fromm, *Man for Himself. An Inquiry into the Psychology of Ethics* (Holt, Rinehart, Winston, New York, 1964).

VI
Successes and Failures
in Human Self-Fulfillment

More traditional terminology for this chapter's title would have been "Virtue and Sin." These words have been avoided purposely because of the connotations which are attached to them. In the traditional understanding of virtue the supernatural aspect received such a heavy emphasis that its human dimension was almost lost. Virtue was seen as a sheer gift of God, and man's contribution to it was restricted mainly to an openness to God's working. In more complete treatises theologians would make a distinction between natural and supernatural virtues to indicate and separate the actions of God and man as two sources in the human self-realization.

In the traditional concept of sin the emphasis was placed on the rejection of God, primarily insofar as God had made his will known in laws or commandments. Sin was exclusively a human activity from which the relationship to God was carefully excluded. Here again, in relation to the human activity, God and man were seen as two separate sources of action, although in relation to sin this separateness was expressed in the total exclusion of God.

In the light of our earlier discussions about the meaning and the task of human life this strong dichotomy seems hardly acceptable. We do not wish to deny the reality of virtue and sin, but virtue and sin are *human* realities. They are forms of human self-realization; they express whether or not man seriously attempts to make his life the living manifestation of God's presence with humanity. Whenever this serious effort is made to the full extent of man's abilities, the human action is successful and the individual's life becomes the manifestation of God's presence with man. This means that man's orientation to the transcendent permeates his whole being and acting. The action is, at the same time, totally the action of God who communicates his own life to man, and it is totally the action of man who makes his own life the living expression of God's presence. There is no dichotomy of a human effort and an additional action of God. When, however, man restricts his own life to his own individual and self-orientated existence, then he eliminates this transcendent dimension from his own being. He fails to be the fullness of human expression, created to the image of God. Self-oriented human existence is still the same complete self-communication of God to humanity in which man receives the power of self-determination, but the action of man doesn't correspond to this gift. The human totality is split into two and the human action in its total perspective is a failure. Complete success and absolute failure seem to be beyond human possibilities. If we admit the exceptions of Christ and the Blessed Virgin, we must say that invariably human action ranges somewhere between the two extremes. No action is totally good, no action is totally evil. The many-sided human reality, as we in fact experience it, will necessarily cause that human action to have some good aspects and others which are less good. This means that every human action contains elements of both success and failure. The traditional terminology of virtue and sin is hardly adequate to describe this full human reality. Let us try to come to a deeper understanding of it here in this study of successes and failures in human self-fulfillment.

I

SUCCESSFUL HUMAN SELF-FULFILLMENT

From the outset we want to make it very clear that in this discussion we are not referring to the purely material success-fulness of human action. Our concern is the human being in his totality and unity. It includes the person (1) as a material existence, (2) in his interpersonal and social relationships, and (3) in his transcendent dimension. There can be human fullness only if these aspects are fully integrated.

The material aspect is not unimportant. It is an essential co-constituent element of earthly human existence. It causes man to be present in time and space, and it is the basis of human communication with all its consequences. But the material aspect alone is not human unless it is made alive by the spiritual aspect of the same reality. The human fullness, however, is only reached when in and through this corporeal-spiritual reality the transcendent dimension of man finds a living expression, as we have tried to explain in Chapters II and III. If, then, we speak here of successful human self-fulfill-ment, we mean that man uses all his material-spiritual capac-ities in a way which is constructively human. In and through this expression his transcendent dimension or his relationship to God receives a concrete and living existence.

From this vantage point we can speak about virtue in the true sense of the word. What we want to point out is that virtue is not something alien to human reality. It is not a suprahuman addition to an already existing human action. Let us use an example. On the staff of a home for emotionally disturbed children there are a number of professional social workers. All their human qualities and professional skill are used to their full extent. They display a patience and con-cern for the welfare of the children which is really edifying, yet they work for a salary and they go home when their work-ing hours are over. It is very doubtful that any of them makes the intention of "doing this for God" or at least for any other "supernatural" purpose. Their whole purpose can be described as an intertwining of human concern and their own need for a salary. Can we speak here of successful human fulfillment? Can we classify their patience and their concern as "virtues" in the traditional sense of the word? Must they add the explicit intention to do this for God in order to make it a real Christian and supernatural virtue? Is it perhaps possible that their actions are "natural" virtues which can be made of "supernatural" value by proper intention? Does the intention shift the value of human actions from "natural" to "super-natural" more or less in the way one goes by a fast elevator from a lower floor to a higher floor? Traditional treatises on virtues, indeed, gave us sometimes (rightly or wrongly) this impression. And if we seem to question the importance of the explicit—or implicit—intention of orienting an action to God, what then is the difference between the value of the human concern expressed by the humanistic atheist and by a deeply religious person?

If we want to arrive at some understanding of this point, we must start by what we can observe in the human action. Every individual person has a certain potential of self-realiza-tion. This potential is deeply influenced by his physical and psychological condition, but despite this conditioning it re-mains a self-potential. It must be activated under the impulse of factors, both from without and from within. This activation is at the same time a new conditioning of the human po-tential, because it creates a certain facility of operation in this specific aspect. It gives a certain "hang toward" or a certain inclination toward this specific form of activation of the hu-man potential. If the same human ability is frequently used in the same manner, the action comes almost "naturally." It becomes "second nature," the normal, easy and almost pre-dictable way of acting for this individual. It is the way in which the self-realization and self-fulfillment of this person takes place. This facility of acting is usually indicated by the term "habit." To the extent that such habits are constructive or destructive for the human *totality*, not simply for the individual, we speak about good and bad habits. St. Thomas Aquinas did the same when he defined virtue as "an operative habit which is good and which brings forth what is good" (*S.T.* I–II, q. 55, a. 3). Here virtue is seen as a truly human quality which relates to human development and self-realization.

However, in this process of self-realization man is not a blind or automatic reactor to impulses and stimuli. A certain form of knowledge enters necessarily into the field. It is man's knowledge that makes acting in this or that manner easier and makes him feel more comfortable. This intertwining of habit and knowledge is for the individual person his form of self-determination. This doesn't mean that he is necessitated to a form of self-expression. For his own benefit or for the welfare of the human community he can adopt a different form of action which might become the beginning of a new habit. Once the facility of acting in this or that way has grown so strong that the action comes almost "naturally," he will only rarely think of why he acts in this specific way. But even under such circumstances we must say that he acts as a human being, that he is responsible for his action, and that he acts "in view of an end." The end which he has in view is his self-fulfillment and self-realization with regard to the human totality. St. Thomas Aquinas and after him almost all theologians give as the specific mark of the human action that man acts "in view of an end." Unfortunately this term "in view of an end" was too often interpreted as an explicit intention. This, however, does not seem to have been what St. Thomas Aquinas had in mind. He saw it rather as an "anthropological" reality, or as something which simply belongs to the human reality. The good habits which are directed to a genuinely constructive human development, individual as well as interpersonal, become then true expressions of successful human self-fulfillment. In traditional terms they may correctly be classified as virtues.

Let us go back to the social workers we have mentioned earlier. We described their attitude as an intertwining of genuine human concern and the personal need for a salary (which is also a form of human concern). Supernatural motives were neither explicitly included nor excluded. Yet we must speak here of successful human self-fulfillment. All their capacities, their personal abilities and professional skill are mobilized for their own development, the benefit of their fellow men and the welfare of their community. It was precisely this kind of setting which Christ described to the disciples of John the Baptist as proof of the presence of the kingdom of God—the blind see, the deaf hear, etc.—namely, the loving concern for human needs. In full human-ness this loving concern is lived in human expression, and in this same human expression it is recognized in its transcendent perspective as the concrete self-manifestation of God's concern in created (communicated) existence. It would seem that this is the fulfillment of man in the totality of his earthly existence. One might say that in this approach we try in a roundabout way to introduce the "good intention" as a specific aspect of the action. In one way this is true, but in another it is not. It is not true insofar as full value of the human action does not require the explicit expression of the transcendent perspective or orientation to God. It is true, however, insofar as the orientation to God—in whatever form this is understood —must be part of man's fundamental option.

If we assume that among the social workers there is one whose intention is very definitely plain selfishness without any real concern for his fellow men, though he puts up an admirable show, then there is a serious defect in his human self-fulfillment. He cuts himself off as a *member* of the human community and reduces the human community to a thing or *object*. Instead of accepting himself as a part of the community, he tries to subject the community to himself. Thus human fullness will not be present, despite the favorable impression which he might create. On the other hand, the explicit intention to work for the sake of God *doesn't make the action virtuous*. The most it can do is deepen the already existing fundamental option or basic tendency of the human activity. An explicit God-orientation is very valuable indeed, and to a greater or lesser degree it is a necessity for every human being to strengthen his basic direction in life, but it is not the magic touch which turns the natural human action into a supernatural performance.

It may seem that we are eliminating the traditional distinction between natural and supernatural virtues. From a certain point of view we do, indeed. We eliminate this distinction insofar as we cannot accept that the same action of genuine human goodness or concern would be a natural virtue in one person and a supernatural virtue in another. Take the example of two nurses in a hospital, having the same dedication, the same unselfish love and concern for their patients. The one lives a "good" life. The other is a prostitute in her spare time. But with regard to their work as professional nurses there is no difference between the two either in dedication or in purpose. Both try honestly to the best of their abilities to be to their patients the expression of God's love and God's concern. To maintain that the dedication of the one has a supernatural value, while the same dedication in the other has a mere natural value, sounds like semantics.

Earlier in this book we discussed how man's orientation to God is not an addition to an already existing human reality. Rather it is the depth-dimension in which the human existence finds its fullness of self-fulfillment. If we want to preserve the distinction between the "natural" and "supernatural"— a distinction that is certainly correct, useful and valuable—

we should see the supernatural as the full development of the "natural." It is not an added quality above the human, but rather the fullness of being human. The Bible teaches us that man was created in the image of God. This means that he reaches the fullness of his "being human" when his life-expression is the manifestation of God's own qualities in human terms. Then his human life is "supernatural," since it is the manifestation of God's active and dynamic presence expressed in human action.

Perhaps people too easily confuse the concept "supernatural" with the idea of "obtaining merits for heaven." "Obtaining merits" is only a consequence, while the concept "supernatural" refers to the source of the action. The source from which the concern for the sick originates in both nurses is their human fullness. This means that they act with their full human capacities, related to the human community as a visible expression of God's own concern for man. What is human nature in them is transformed into being a self-expression of God, without ceasing to be fully human.

This also shows that, from another point of view, we do not eliminate the distinction between natural and supernatural. There can be human actions which are not the manifestation of God's presence with man. Christ spoke about this in Matthew 6:1: "Be careful not to parade your good deeds before men to attract their notice; by doing this you will lose all your reward from your Father in heaven." The meaning seems clear. If the sole purpose of the human activity is to project one's own self rather than to let one's human reality be the manifestation of God's presence in human life, the human action does not reach its fullness and transformation, while on the other hand in "sinners" this same transformation can be a concrete reality. Christ indicates this when he says: "Her many sins must have been forgiven her, or she would not have shown such great love" (Lk. 7:47). In the sinful woman,

despite her many aberrations, human fullness in its deepest
dimension was a concrete reality. This transformed her life
and made her "pleasing to God."

The Intertwining of the Divine and Human as
One Source of Action

Above we described the supernatural as the depth-dimension and the fullness of human existence, and not as a special,
God-given addition to human reality. It may seem to some
that we deviate from the traditional approach to this matter
in theology. Through the ages theologians have spoken about
"habits" which are acquired by human action and development, while other habits are "infused" by God. St. Thomas
Aquinas speaks very clearly about virtues as "qualities of inner
goodness through which one lives well, which cannot be used
in an evil way and which God produces in us without our
cooperation" (S.T. I–II, q. 55, a. 4). Especially the words
"which God produces in us without our cooperation" may
seem to imply that according to "solid theology" we must see
certain "habits" as special gifts of God, and not merely as a
depth-dimension of human reality. Such a view almost entails
that the virtuous human action comes from a double source,
the human and the divine.

However, this was not what St. Thomas Aquinas had in
mind. He did not see as a contradiction that the same human
habit could be the source of an action which is truly the
manifestation of God's presence with man. First he makes
clear what he means by "infused habit." Infused habit is not
the same as "going beyond human capacities." If a person
who never studied any foreign language would suddenly speak
correctly a difficult foreign language, this would not be an infused habit. It would merely be the strengthening of an

existing human habit, because knowledge of languages is not outside the human realm. We may speak about a special intervention of God, but not about an infused habit (*S.T.* I–II, q. 51, a. 4 ad 3). Only when the object of the action itself goes beyond the possibilities of a created existence can we speak of an infused habit. For example, to love God and to be actively the living self-manifestation of God in created existence goes beyond created claims. The effect as well as the source of love must be produced by God (*S.T.* I–II, q. 51, a. 4).

But this does not mean that we must accept a double source of action in the performance of virtues. There is only one source. It is the human source elevated and transformed to be the expression of God's presence with man. In its totality it is a gift of God, but it is no less totally human. It is precisely this that God created man to be—created in the image of God. It is precisely this that Christ came to reveal when he described his task as "to expand what had been hidden from the foundation of the world" (Mt. 13:12). It was also this message, hidden for centuries and generations but now revealed to the saints, which St. Paul preached. He calls it "the mystery of God with you. . . . The reality of it is Christ" (Col. 2:17). Thus the infused habit is not a distinct reality from the acquired or human habit, but the depth-dimension in which the fullness of creation is finally reached.

When we speak about successes in human self-fulfillment, then the human relationship with God is included in this expression. Whether it is explicitly accepted or not, the human fullness is by its nature the self-manifestation of the divine in created and perceptible form. When theologians divide the habits, as sources of action, into categories of acquired and infused, then they are speaking about the same human reality, but from a different point of view. Insofar as a habit is man's activity and self-development, it is acquired;

insofar as it manifests God's living presence, it is infused. But in its totality it is the one gift of God who made man in his own image.

Divine Reality and Human Expression

The intertwining of the divine and the human is essential if we want to understand how the same action can be simultaneously human self-fulfillment and self-manifestation of God. To be this living self-manifestation of God is to participate to a certain degree in the life of God. Yet we may not say that this participation is the same as identification with God. Although God manifests himself in creation, creation—and man—may not be identified with God. By comparison we may say that a composer expresses his skill, his feelings, his mood and his personality in a piece of music, yet the composition may not be identified with the author. God has granted to man to participate in his life and to activate this participation in human actions, yet these human actions may not be simply identified with the actions of God. They are a "participation," the divine reality in human expression.

For centuries Christian theology has made a distinction between divine virtues and moral virtues precisely to indicate the human and the divine dimension of the same reality. This distinction emphasizes at the same time that the divine and the human are not identical. The proper characteristic of the human task is that man is personally responsible for making his own life the manifestation of God's presence. He does so by the activation of his human qualities in the situation of his own existence. This personal existence of man is the human perspective of his life. It is concerned with the potential which he has, with the use and the development of this potential in which its relation to others and the well-being of others must be taken into account. In this perspective the focus of the attention is geared toward what is within the reach of human reality itself. This focus, however, does not exclude the God-oriented dimension in man, but rather it considers where and how this orientation to God must come to life. It is here that theology speaks of moral virtues.

But the same human activity is imbued and made alive by God's self-communication to man. This self-communication is not a superimposed quality which either adds something to the human reality or eliminates the human perspective of the action. It leaves to the human action its full human value and transforms this human value in its totality. This transformation causes the human action to be a true self-manifestation of God. This transformation or depth-dimension does not come to man despite himself or against his will. Although it is purely a gift of God to man, man himself is actively involved in achieving this transformation. This human involvement and activity in which the focus falls totally upon the man-God relationship is indicated by the term "theological or divine virtues." The distinction between theological and moral virtues is, therefore, as valid and as important today as it was in the past. Perhaps more emphasis is placed today upon the unified approach to human life and upon the essential connection and interaction of the virtues. Perhaps we may come to greater clarity if we consider the theological virtues of faith, hope and charity in more detail.

The triad faith, hope and charity goes back to apostolic times. Though the words and perhaps the concepts are different, they actually refer to three different aspects of the same reality. They describe the human reality as it sees itself as dependent on and related to God. None of them can be living and real without the actual presence of the other two.

It is a characteristic of man to have a measure of insight into the nature and purpose of his own being. This insight is not a mere intellectualization. His human urges and desires play a role in helping him understand the presence of a power beyond his own reach. This power escapes comprehension, yet it presents itself as deeply personal. It is beyond all measurement and imagination, yet its being is encountered undivided in man's own limited being. It is no obstacle to man's personal and free self-expression, yet man perceives it as an all-pervading influence which marks the realization of his self. This all-encompassing presence is recognized as the source of his own being and as the perspective which gives meaning and depth to man's interpersonal expression. Man recognizes the transcendent perspective of his own being and accepts the transcendent itself as the source and fulfillment of his own existence. He cannot strictly prove it; he must accept it. He knows that he accepts it on his own responsibility, yet he knows also that not accepting this transcendent being would mean that he is not true to himself. Man sees and accepts himself as coming forth from God, as being totally dependent on God. God is not understood as the master who commands and rules from without, but as the center and core of man's own being. This is a faith which is alive.

Precisely in the recognition of the transcendent presence of God and in the immanence of the divine within himself, man can see his own limitations. But the experience of these limitations is not a paralyzing fear. It does not prevent man from recognizing and accepting his own abilities. On the contrary, the acceptance of the immanent and transcendent presence of God fills him with confidence that this same God who is the source of his limited being will also be the source of strength which enables him to fulfill his expectations. The presence of the transcendent is experienced as an essential perspective in human existence, but, therefore, also the assistance of the transcendent creator is seen by man as more than a mere expectation. This assistance is part of his own being. Human hope is at the same time a certainty and a security. However, man knows that it does not dispense him from activating all his human abilities.

Faith and hope will be fruitful realities only when they are actively expressed in man's human surrender to the transcendent power and presence of God. Then man's human activity becomes the expression of this presence. All human abilities are then evaluated and actively employed to make the total expression of human life the perceptible presence of the transcendent itself. This surrender to the transcendent is the active recognition that human life and existence are a gift of God. We don't deny that human existence has a value of its own, but in faith and hope this same human existence and this same human expression are recognized and accepted as the manifestation of the creator. This active acceptance means a personal surrender of man to God. We call this "love" or "charity." In this surrender man expresses his active concern for being God's self-manifestation and he makes his respect for God a living reality. This love or this active response to God is the final establishment of the human relationship with God. In this relationship, faith and hope evaluate God's existence and the human reality in their deepest dimension, although it is only in love that they find their ultimate fulfillment. This seems to be what St. Paul said: "There are three things that last: faith, hope and love; and the greatest of these is love" (1 Cor. 13:13). When St. Thomas Aquinas called charity the form of all virtues, he meant that, in and because of charity only, every virtue becomes a virtue.

But this triad—faith, hope, love—is a unity. If either one is lacking the others cannot exist or at least cannot be alive. It is in the unified presence of these three that God communicates himself to man. It is, thus, in the presence of these three that human existence becomes the living manifestation of God's presence in creation. It is thus that man participates in the life of God. This fullness of human expression is totally a divine gift, but is also totally a human response for which man himself is responsible, and from which he has the power to withdraw. Man can refuse to believe and to accept the transcendent perspective and value of his own life. Man can make the tangible world, his own benefit and pleasure, or the human community to be the purpose and fulfillment of his existence. In their visible human expression the difference between pure humanism and God-orientation may often not be perceptible. The difference lies in the intangibles of faith, hope and love. Where these are present we accept the participation in the life of God, which we call sanctifying grace. It is again this basic orientation to God, the transcendent perspective of the human reality, which makes every human action the manifestation of God's presence. This is perhaps best summarized by James Gustafson in *Christ and the Moral Life*: "The sanctifying grace of God shapes the Christian life so that the activities of man are brought into conformity to the grace they receive, and so that the particular moral virtues and actions are governed and directed by this grace." [1]

II
FAILURE IN HUMAN SELF-FULFILLMENT

We use the expression "Failure in Human Self-Fulfillment" to avoid the word "sin," which has so many unfortunate connotations. These connotations we can easily see in the traditional definition of "sin" as a willful transgression of the law of God. We do not question the accuracy of this definition but we may not overlook its disadvantages. If we describe sin as a willful transgression of the law of God, then we are inclined to think of two rather independent realities. One is the law of God which is then understood as an outline of conduct which has been handed down to man from above; the other is the rebellious human performance. This makes us think of sin as a static reality. But sin is not static; it is a dynamic aspect of human existence. Sin is a deformity in the expression of the transcendent dimension of human self-realization. This dynamic aspect we want to bring to the foreground.

We have no doubt about the existence of the law of God, but this law of God is not an externally imposed outline of human behavior. God's law rather is the dynamic force for self-realization that he has placed in the potential of the human totality. This human potential contains an immense range of possible actions and responses. It is within this range of possibilities that lies man's task to give a concrete expression to his own individual self in relation to the material world and the human community. The whole realm of physical dispositions, mental capacities, environmental conditions and cultural patterns plays its role in human self-expression. The law of God is contained in this same totality. It is not an outline or a description. It is the dynamic need for creative and constructive realization of this total perspective.

In this context sin may still be defined as a transgression of God's law, but it may not be seen as a comparison between the human performance and a pre-established outline of conduct. The emphasis must fall on the human self-realization. God did not command any specific human action. He gave to man the task to activate his potential creatively and constructively in the total human perspective. Sin enters into the field when the human activity fails to take into account all the essential elements of self-realization. This means that we can speak of sin only when man does not fulfill any aspect of his own potential that he ought to fulfill—for example, when he disregards the creative and constructive building of the human community, when he exploits others for his own benefit, when he endangers his own life or the life of others without necessity, etc.

Thus it becomes extremely difficult to speak of specific actions as always sinful. We are so used to saying that "stealing" or "lying" or "killing an innocent person" is always sinful. In ordinary conversation we identify these concepts with "taking something which is not ours" or "giving information which we know is not true" or "taking the life of a person who has committed no crime against us." The material dimension of the action is then readily qualified as sin. But sin is then too easily placed outside the concrete human expression as an objective "thing" that man may not perform. In fact, however, stealing and lying are not "things" that exist until human self-realization fails to fulfill itself constructively in relation to the human community.

This failure in self-fulfillment is a failure in man's relationship with God, for man must be God's image precisely in his human self-expression. The reality of sin exists only in the reality of the human relationship with God. In *Morality for Our Time* Marc Oraison says: "The word 'sin' is a technical term designating a reality which is at once precise and complex, namely, the concrete situation of individual man or humanity as a whole at a particular stage in their *real* relationship to a living and personal God." [2] If Oraison's description is right, we must accept that sin is a failure in human self-fulfillment. The real relationship to a living and personal God is the human person expressing himself in the realization of his own potential in a creative and constructive relationship to the human community. God is here not an onlooker who stays at the outside as ruler and commander. God is the one whose inner self is made perceptible in this reality in a created and limited way. Where man fails in his self-fulfillment in this total perspective, there he fails to give perceptible expression to the presence of the living and personal God. This is sin.

In Chapter IV we described God's law as the successful human self-realization. The formulated law is a description of the values which the individual must express in concrete and living form. Not the letter, but the value itself, is the important aspect. The history of revelation clearly shows that throughout the developmental stages of man's understanding of his relationship with God human self-fulfillment or the lack thereof was the foundation of the concepts of good and evil.

Let us try to summarize briefly what the Old and New Testaments teach us on this point.

Sin as Failure of Human Self-Fulfillment in the Old Testament

The Old Testament presents a great variety and multiplicity of commandments. In many instances we see how the chosen people were punished by God because of their transgression of his laws. This may easily mislead us and make us think that for the Hebrews sinfulness was the same as a transgression of a formulated law. Such an understanding is totally unjustified. The prophet Isaiah reproached them very explicitly: "Yahweh has said: 'Because this people approaches me only in words, honors me only with lip-service while its heart is far from me, and my religion, as far as it is concerned, is nothing but human commandments, a lesson memorized, very well, I shall have to go on being prodigal of prodigious prodigies with this people. The wisdom of its sages shall decay, the intelligence of its intelligent men shall be shrouded'" (Is. 29:13–14).

The prophet did not speak primarily about a lack of observance of the formulated laws. On the contrary, he reproached them for overemphasizing the value of the formulation at the cost of the deeper human and God-related value which the laws tried to express. Religion was not a living reality but a "lesson memorized." Therefore it had no value before Yahweh.

The Old Testament expresses the concept of sin in a variety of words and of meanings. But whatever word or meaning is used, it always refers to a failure in interhuman relationship, and in this failure God is offended. So sin is recognized in the disloyalty to the agreement between a lord and his servant, in the failure of a subject to fulfill his obligation, in the failure of the host to fulfill his duty of hospitality, in the rebellion of the child against his father, etc. However, not only positively harmful actions are classified as sins, but also the failure to act and not to live up to one's potential. By action or by non-action one can cause a situation which "ought not to exist." Such distortion caused by the agent is not only a guilt before Yahweh, but a lack of self-fulfillment which causes rejection by God.

The prophet Jeremiah warns that "the sin of Judah is written with an iron pen . . . on the tablet of their heart . . . as evidence against them" (Jer. 17:1). The prophet Ezekiel compares the sinful city of Jerusalem with a "rusty cooking-pot," but "all that rust will not disappear in the flames. I have tried to purge you of the filth of your debauchery, but you would not let yourself be purged of your filth. So you will not be purged until my anger has been exhausted against you. I, Yahweh, have spoken" (Ez. 24:12–13).

The actions and the words of the prophets reproach much more than mere transgressions of formulated laws. They describe a distortion in the human reality which does not any longer reflect God's presence with man. For the Hebrews the formulated law itself was the embodiment of their covenant with Yahweh. In the law Yahweh made himself perceptibly present to his people, and in the observance of the law they became in reality the people of God. The covenant between Yahweh and his people was introduced with these words: "From this you know that now, if you obey my voice and hold fast to my covenant, you of all the nations shall be my very own, for all the earth is mine. I will count you a kingdom of priests, a consecrated nation" (Ex. 19:5).

The covenant was given in the form of laws; in the observance of the laws the people would become a "consecrated nation." Then the law itself received a personal perspective as a value-representation which entered into the very being of the personal fulfillment of the people. The transgression of the law was a personal affront to Yahweh, but also a lack of self-fulfillment of those who had accepted the covenant. The law was the manifestation of Yahweh's presence with the people; the observance of the law made Yahweh's presence a living reality. The failure to give concrete expression to this living presence was human sinfulness.

This becomes more evident when we consider that the center of all sinfulness in the Old Testament is the sin of idolatry. The exiles and other hardships which the people suffered were almost invariably a consequence of and a punishment for idolatry. The ten commandments are introduced with a statement of Yahweh's authority: "I am Yahweh your God who brought you out of the land of Egypt, out of the house of slavery. You shall have no other gods except me" (Ex. 21:1). All the commandments that follow concerning the worship of Yahweh and interhuman relationships find their basis and meaning in this one statement. The transgression of any of those commandments would be equivalent to a refusal to acknowledge the supremacy of Yahweh.[3] Yahweh had to be accepted as the only and one God. He was totally free and independent, not subject to fate as the gods of other nations. No other being could be the competitor of Yahweh. His presence and sovereignty had to be reflected in human attitudes and behavior. Man's self-expression had to be the realization of the potential which Yahweh had entrusted to human responsibility. It was a gift of God to man.

In many instances it happened that man overlooked how his whole being had a value of its own while remaining totally a gift of Yahweh. Then he created his own gods, and by magical rites he tried to secure for himself certain powers which were divine. In his desire to be mighty and great he projected his wish into a god who was a mighty ruler. He subjected himself to this god and in magical rites he tried to please him, and, possibly, to participate in this power and claim divinity for himself. The unknown and awe-inspiring powers of life and procreation were projected into a god of fertility. In magical rites again man made the effort to secure these powers for himself and to share in this divine quality. Thus we see in the Old Testament how the anger of Yahweh arose when his people went to the heights of Baal and participated in the pagan rites. This was much more than the transgression of a formulated law. The acceptance of "strange gods" was a refusal to accept Yahweh as the sovereign giver of all things. People turned themselves and raised their own desires and urges to a status of divinity. Their attitudes and behavior became a deification and adoration of their own inner self. Thus man lost his freedom and became a slave of his own instinctual drives. It was a distortion of what man ought to be in the eyes of Yahweh.

The accusations and warnings of the prophets were repeatedly directed against the hardening of the heart: "If only you would listen to him today. Don't harden your hearts as at Meribah, as you did that day at Massah [place of temptation] in the wilderness" (Ps. 95:8). It is man's own responsibility to be open to God's teaching; nonetheless, this openness remains a gift of God, as Isaiah implies when he prays: "Why, Yahweh, leave us to stray from your ways and harden our hearts against fearing you?" (Is. 63:17). But the hardening of the heart against Yahweh is also the reason why they will not receive their own fullness and happiness. The psalmist says it in this way: "For forty years that generation repelled me, until I said: How unreliable these people who refuse to grasp my ways! And so, in anger, I swore that not one would reach the place of rest I had for them" (Ps. 95:10–11).

In the Old Testament sin is the refusal to acknowledge the name of God. It is the rejection of the personal relationship with God which manifests itself in individual behavior and interhuman relationship.

Sin as Failure of Human Self-Fulfillment
in the New Testament

The Old Testament knew God as the liberator and lawgiver. Man was made free from slavery, and this freedom had to be manifested in the fulfillment of God's commandments. God's presence with man, man's self-fulfillment and the fulfillment of God's commandments fused into one concrete expression. In the New Testament the understanding of God's presence with man developed into a deeper person-to-person relationship of God with man in the person of Christ. Christ was at the same time the living reality of God's personal presence with humanity and the message to every individual human being that he was called to personal participation in the life and self-manifestation of God in humanity. This deeper understanding of God's personal self-manifestation in humanity gives a special perspective to the meaning of human self-realization. But also, it gives a special depth to the meaning of sin as failure of human self-fulfillment.

The difference between the Old and New Testaments is not primarily a matter of different realities, but rather a difference in the depth-dimension of one and the same reality. Christ came "not to abolish," but "to expound what had been hidden from the foundation of the world." In the Old Testament human self-fulfillment was manifested in dependence on God's law; God's presence was made visible in man's obedience. In the New Testament human self-fulfillment is destined to be a personal participation in the inner life of God. In this light, the failure of human self-fulfillment goes far beyond a failure to acknowledge God's supremacy. It is the refusal to make the personal life of God a living reality in human existence.

In the teaching of Christ we find references to sin as individual human actions, as in his answer to the adulterous woman: "Go away and don't sin anymore" (Jn. 8:11). But Christ expressed the heart of his teaching at the beginning of his ministry where he said: "Repent, and believe the Good News" (Mk. 1:15). The repentance which Christ preached was the complete change of heart, the redirection of human attitudes because of the Good News of the messianic fulfillment. It was the message of Christ that human reality is destined to be the living expression of God's presence with us. To reject this message willfully is to stay in a sinful condition: "Blind? If you were you would not be guilty, but since you say, 'we see,' your guilt remains" (Jn. 9:41). C. Spicq[4] points out that the "sin that is death" is the "christological sin," that is, the rejection of Christ as the self-revelation of God, for "anyone who does not believe God is making God out to be a liar" (1 Jn. 5:10). On various occasions Christ pointed out that the external observance of the laws is not the most important factor in man's justification, but what comes forth from the heart defiles man. In the parable of the prodigal son Christ gives us the message that no specific action constitutes his sinfulness. The sinfulness of this young man consists in his self-seeking attitude in which he isolates himself from the community to which he belongs.[5]

In the epistles of St. John sin is called "lawlessness" and "unrighteousness" which comes forth from the "sensual body, the lustful eye, and pride in possessions" (1 Jn. 2:16). He doesn't exclude the possible sinfulness of individual actions, but focuses on the total human approach to life. Sinfulness is the human failure to respond to the task which has been entrusted to him.

In the teaching of St. Paul it becomes even clearer how much the service of God is an essential aspect of human existence. St. Paul rejects explicitly the idea that the law itself contributes anything to justification. The law only outlines the direction in which man must seek the fulfillment of his vocation, and it makes him aware of his limitations and of his sinfulness. Even without a formulated law, by his very existence man knows that he is subject to the demands of the creator. Speaking about pagans who do not know the law of Moses, St. Paul says: "In other words, since they refused to see it was rational to acknowledge God, God left them to their own irrational ideas and to their monstrous behavior. . . . They know what God's verdict is: that those who behave like this deserve to die—and yet they do it; and what is worse, encourage others to do the same" (Rom. 1:28–32). Their sinfulness is pictured in verses 29 and 30, but the core of this sinfulness is their refusal to acknowledge God, as Paul had said a little earlier: "They have exchanged the glory of the immortal God for a worthless imitation, for the image of mortal man. . . . That is why God has left them to their filthy enjoyments . . . since they have given up divine truth for a lie and have worshiped and served creatures instead of the creator" (Rom. 1:23–25).

The submission to human passions and domination by their own lust and urges is presented here as being for them and expression of religion. At the same time it is a sort of idolatry, for it is always an adoration of self, even if only in one's body.[6] When St. Paul speaks about sin and sinfulness, he certainly refers to individual actions, but these actions are the result of a deeper human tendency. Sinfulness is a personal responsibility in which man refuses to accept his life as a task to be a personal manifestation of the creator; instead he searches for his own satisfaction, while rejecting the relationship to God.

However, for St. Paul sin is not only an individual action or a personal attitude of the human being. Sin is also a human condition which reigns as a power in this world. It affects all mankind, as St. Paul says: "Yet death reigned over all from Adam to Moses, even though their sin, unlike that of Adam, was not a matter of breaking a law" (Rom.

5:14). Sin is seen as a power which holds all humanity in its grip. Its beginning is traced back to the origin of mankind. The first chapters of Genesis are not a narration of material happenings in the past, but a theological reflection upon the condition of man. It pictures the human condition as an expression of disobedience to God. To obey means to respond to the call of God which is contained in creation. Sin, as we see this in the action of Adam, is precisely a refusal to give this response.[7] Every human being who is born into this world is born into this condition and is subject to it because he belongs to the human race.

Every human being in the totality of his earthly existence is inclined to sin. St. Paul speaks about "the body as it is inclined to sin," the *soma tes hamartias* (Rom. 5:6)[8] in which man necessarily exists, but which does not take away his responsibility. St. Paul finds in every man an ambivalent striving. He is called to an intimate relationship with the creator, yet he rejects responding to this call. It is this condition that St. Augustine described as "original sin." One might say that original sin describes in a negative way the core of the Christian message, while the New Testament proclaims the Christian message in a positive way. Original sin, in its deepest meaning, does not point to a moral fault or to an actual happening in the past, but rather is a description of the miserable condition of unredeemed mankind, an interpretation of the unredeemed human reality in the light of the message of salvation.[9]

The New Testament announces in a positive way the message of salvation where it speak of the incarnation, of the life and the teachings of Christ. It is a message of grace and mercy, but it also says that man is blind and deaf and lame and sick, etc. It does not indicate that the message of God's love and merciful concern is primarily directed to those who suffer these physical discomforts. But it does express that mankind was blind and deaf and lame in the light of what

God had prepared for man and to what man was called to be. The paralyzed man was healed after his sins had been forgiven (Lk. 5:20) and the man who was blind from birth had been born in this condition "so that the works of God might be displayed in him" (Jn. 9:3). The message of the Gospels is a message of life and healing. This message brings the transition from the unredeemed human condition to the full unfolding of man's vocation.

Thus the Scriptures, the Old Testament as well as the New Testament, understand sin as a human reality in which man in his earthly condition positively refuses to respond to God's invitation. The power of self-realization, which is the proper task of man, is used negatively. It is a deceptive self-fulfillment which in fact leads to self-destruction. It is the refusal to be the image of the living God. In its deepest meaning sin is death.

Sin as a Human Reality

There is no precise outline for the human task of self-fulfillment, but this task must continuously be discovered. Every human being must gain by insight into what his capacities are; he must come to understand what contributes to their unfolding and how this unfolding affects the human community. Finally he must see how his influence upon the human community has its repercussions upon his own further personal development. This is not a matter of purely intellectual insight. It involves the whole person with all his intellectual, emotional and physical qualities.

Such a complete personal involvement is a complicated matter. Human knowledge is strongly dependent on man's physical condition, especially on that of the brain, and is also greatly influenced by cultural patterns and opportunities for learning. The volitional and emotional capacities of each individual not only are influenced by his intellectual capacities, but they are profoundly affected by the physical condition of the person and by all the environmental relationships which he has experienced. Instinctual drives easily obscure the development of insight, and personal needs easily guide a person into a certain direction of self-realization. Cooperation of the community can open new vistas for the unfolding of the individual, but the resistance of one's fellow men may close the way to any form of personal progress.

From every point of view the human capacities are limited and conditioned by circumstances which are beyond the individual's control. However, these limitations and conditions do not prevent a personal responsibility. It is precisely the human task to search for possible forms of self-realization within the situation in which an individual finds himself. When the disadvantageous situation cannot be changed, it must be incorporated into the personal self-expression. Human reality comes into being in the interplay of a free self-determination on the basis of one's insight into his actual situation. In traditional terminology we may call this the interaction between knowledge and free will. In either perspective man can fail. He may fall short in his search for insight and let himself be driven by his instinctual urges or selfish inclinations. Or he may have sufficient insight but lack the courage or the will to apply himself to the task which he knows to be his. Failure in human self-fulfillment doesn't result from a comparison between actual performance and an abstract ideal. There is failure when the performance doesn't measure up to the potential which the individual has and to the constructive realization of this potential.

It was not uncommon in the past, and perhaps it is not yet uncommon today, for people to look at saints as examples of sanctity and perfection. But instead of studying how a saint activated his potential in his personal life-expression, they try to imitate his material activity. They will fail, of course, and make themselves ridiculous. They overlook that the external performances of a saint make sense only as a realization of his potential, which was different from the potential of everyone else.

The boy who takes an athlete as his idol will study the techniques of his sport and try to express this technique with his own abilities. Mere dreaming about his hero will get him nowhere and will only lead to discouragement. This discouragement would be caused by the boy's own mistake, since he did not take a hard look at his own potential or make the effort to use the potential he has. Knowledge and will are interrelated, yet they are not the same. In either aspect the human being may fail by his own fault. Therefore, it will be useful to study them separately, provided we keep in mind that in every act of knowledge the will is present; similarly, no genuine act of the will is possible without a certain amount of knowledge.

1. *Knowledge and Human Self-Fulfillment.* It is characteristic of man not to be driven by blind instinct, but to direct himself toward his goal. This doesn't mean total independence, however. Man is subject to many limitations which are beyond his control. Some of these limitations are pre-given; others are created by himself or by his fellow men. Man's self-direction can only take place within the boundaries of these limitations. Self-direction demands knowledge; it is not only a matter of having a certain goal before one's eyes, for a certain understanding of one's capacities is also required.

However, if the development of the human capacities is to lead to a truly human self-fulfillment, it is subject to many other conditions. The well-being of other individuals and of the human community plays an important role. An individual development which is primarily self-oriented and disregards others may lead to a high form of development of a specific human capacity, but it can fall short in an essential aspect of the total human value, namely, in the interhuman relationship. The knowledge required for a well-balanced and integrated human self-fulfillment is a very complex affair. The multi-faceted dimensions of human existence make it almost impossible for the individual to oversee at once all the dimensions of his activity.

If we want to have an action which is completely and fully an expression of the total person, then we would have to include in it the simultaneous understanding and awareness of all his abilities, of the place of this ability or action in his totality, of the impact of the action on others, of the repercussion of this impact upon himself, and in this totality his relationship to God. But human knowledge is partial. It is tied to the senses and developed in the experiences of life. The human mind can truly concentrate on only very few things at the same time. All the other dimensions are more or less present in the form of attitudes which man has created within himself.

Take the example of a teacher. If he wants to convey his knowledge to his students in the classroom, his mind is totally occupied with the problem which he presents to his class. All the other aspects, such as his interest in the subject, his concern for the students, the fact that he sees teaching as his vocation in life, the care and love for the family at home, the personality development of his students and his own growth through the interaction between the students and himself, and in this total perspective his own relationship to God—all these aspects are present. But the presence of these aspects is not an awareness. It is rather an attitudinal condition which expresses itself in his present activity. Only once in a while does the value of his activity dawn upon him in a veiled way in all its various dimensions. This may happen when he sits back and reflects upon his own life, or on rare occasions it may happen at a certain moment while he is teaching. On such occasions the value of his actions unfolds itself before him as completely as this is possible in his human condition. Then also is he able to say a full "yes" or "no" to his human self-realization.

Such moments are essential elements in the formation of human attitudes. These attitudes account for his "being-as-a-whole" to be involved in his individual action. It is in this vision on the whole life and on the person's self-fulfillment that the individual action transcends its isolated individuality. Human self-fulfillment and working toward a goal then become an anthropological reality which is present in every individual action. In every action man then says to a certain extent "yes" or "no" to his self-fulfillment, and, through this self-fulfillment, to his relationship with God.

Because of the limitations and of the ambivalence of human existence, man is necessarily confronted with a choice in most of his actions. In almost every decision he is aware of the fact that there are both desirable and undesirable elements or consequences. For example, dedication to a teaching career puts demands on time and energy—perhaps on the time which he thinks he should spend with his family. A physician may feel obliged to spend so much time on his patients that his own family suffers harm. The businessman may have to move so often from one location to another that his children can never find the security of a familiar school and neighborhood environment. The physician's concern for his patients and the businessman's prospects for a better job are contributive to their self-development and self-fulfillment, but at the same time the harm this does to their family impedes their development as total persons. Every decision implies a risk which only can be met in a total and comprehensive knowledge or an intuitive vision of the total human condition. But such a vision is beyond the reach of man's present condition.

The same lack of total knowledge exists with respect to the

human action which seems to run contrary to authentic human self-development, the sinful action. The activity of a traitor must certainly be considered most harmful to the community. Yet in the mind of the traitor there is a certain amount of good in his action. He may even be honestly convinced that he does the right thing. He may be enticed by personal gain, or he may act to revenge injustice which he suffered in his own nation, or perhaps his family is kept as hostages. Understanding his action in all its human depth would demand that all of its possible implications be understood. But this again is beyond grasp of the human condition on earth where man can only work with limited and partial insights. Although his action expresses that his self-fulfillment took a negative and harmful direction which leads to self-destruction, his "yes" or "no" to his action was based upon partial insight only and therefore is by its nature not irrevocable.

As long as man lives on earth, certain constructive and harmful elements are always interwoven in his actions. To what extent he can avoid these harmful elements, or to what extent he has planned them purposely, or to what extent they are the result of earlier formation or lack of formation, is a matter that is difficult to determine.

Moral theology has traditionally taught that it is necessary to have full knowledge to commit a "mortal sin." Considered in the light of the preceding reflections, one may wonder what this "full knowledge" means. And we may wonder what "mortal sin" really means. Traditionally it is understood as a "total rejection of God" or as the "complete loss of the friendship of God," the loss of sanctifying grace. But when human knowledge with regard to a particular action is so rarely the expression of the *total* human reality, and when every action has a certain perspective of "constructive self-fulfillment," then it becomes very difficult to speak of a total rejection of God, especially in a single action. If the fundamental orientation of a person is positive and constructive, then a single action cannot cause a sudden and complete change. The action may be seriously harmful and destructive, but it is not a total change of personal value, nor is it irrevocable. An irrevocable condition exists only in death.

Since in every human action desirable and undesirable elements are interwoven, it will be impossible to call some actions totally good and others totally evil. Rather the extreme opposites shall be seen as follows. Some actions are mostly good and slightly harmful, while other actions are slightly good and mostly harmful. The majority of the human actions are somewhere in between these extremes. The moral value of human actions covers a wide grey area. A demarcation line between "venial" sins and "mortal" sins cannot ever be drawn with any degree of accuracy. Even if human insight tells us that an action is evil, its "evilness" is still very different from an irrevocable decision. Perhaps we should speak with Piet Schoonenberg of a threefold division of sins, namely, venial sin, mortal sin and sin unto death. In venial sin man is aware of and consents to the slightly harmful elements in his actions, though he could avoid them to a certain extent. In mortal sin he gives his consent to greatly harmful effects which he could avoid, while the sin unto death contains the final rejection of his ultimate self-fulfillment.

2. Self-Determination and Human Self-Fulfillment. The above-discussed complexity in relation to knowledge and human self-fulfillment holds also for self-determination. Perhaps it is even more complicated in this respect. In many aspects of his life man is not under control of his intellectual insight. His emotions and feelings play an important role in almost all his decisions. Man's power of self-determination, which we have described in Chapter III, does not simply flow forth from his cognitive faculties alone. Self-determination means the activation of the personal "self" to give expression to something considered to be a value. A value may be described as a good which contributes to the fulfillment of a person's needs. Even the masochistic search for self-punishment contains a good in the eyes of the person who searches for it. A personal need goes beyond one's intellectual understanding, at least in many respects. One's whole physiological composition and instinctual urges, one's facility of action on certain points, and early life experiences of acceptance and rejection, of frustration and success in one's personal endeavors and interhuman relationships—all these create in the individual certain needs which partly escape intellectual insight and control. Not only do they often escape insight and control, but they may also give a certain direction to one's insight. They may cause the individual to see things in a specific way.

In man's needs and emotions human ambivalence strongly manifests itself. Everyone experiences the need to be himself, that is, the need to be independent. But he also experiences the needs of other people, and this means that there is a need for dependence. Early life experiences have taught the person a certain form of balance which he sees as valid for his own personality. This particular and individual balance indicates the proportion between his concern for self and his concern for others and the community. Later development, increasing insight and knowledge will give a special shape to this balance, but the earliest foundation of it cannot be completely taken away.

Based upon these needs and in conjunction with his intellectual insights, man can develop a realistic ideal of self-realization. This realistic ideal is often different from the ego-ideal or the wish-fulfillment which results from one's inner needs. It takes into account the interpersonal perspectives, and it has the courage to restrain unrealistic wishes for the sake of a fuller self-fulfillment. We must repeat again that these inner urges are only partly under the control of the person. The least they always do is to create a tendency in the human being which gives a certain color and flavor to the insights which he develops. They give a certain direction to his inclinations. They give a feeling of well-being when they are fulfilled. However, at the same time they allow contrary inclinations and urges, so that a clear "yes" or "no" is impossible in many instances.

The clearest example of this is perhaps the feeling of a teenager toward his parents. As a rule we may say that the youngster loves his parents and that he has a fairly good idea why he must respect them. He feels that his parents intend to do what is best for their children, but at the same time he deeply resents being under their control. A fifteen-year-old boy said during a counseling session that he thought that his father was a pretty good guy: "He means well, but I hate the way he is always on my back. If he would give me a chance to be myself, I would behave differently and be less rebellious." Apart from all other good or bad qualities which this boy may possess, it became very clear that he wanted his father's guidance and advice but at the same time not his father's mold. It obviously is extremely difficult to indicate exactly where or when "rebellion" is good or evil. There is almost always a mixture of legitimate and necessary self-fulfillment and an unbalanced self-concern which leads to a lack of respect for the human community.

Since the fulfillment of God's law coincides with the proper self-fulfillment of man in the perspective of his total existence, we find in almost every human action certain elements which are in accordance with God's law and elements which are contrary to it. To make a judgment on the moral value of the human action is, therefore, an almost impossible task. Our judgment can only be based upon external factors which can never totally disclose the hidden depths of human urges and needs. This may become clearer if we concentrate for a moment on evident harmful aspects of a certain action, for instance, the act of adultery. Obviously we don't intend to condone it or to minimize its seriousness. In the example we have in mind the woman committed adultery and became pregnant in this extra-marital affair.

She had married her husband about ten years before, and it was his second marriage. He had divorced his first wife because she got pregnant while he was overseas in the service. Before his second marriage he had made it very clear to his wife-to-be that she would get no chance to play the same "trick" on him as his first wife had done. She would have no telephone, no car, no tea parties with other women, no trips to town for any reason except in his company, etc. In brief, she was completely "confined to quarters" if he wasn't with her. For the first few years everything was fine, but in the course of time loneliness caught up with her, especially since he was often away on lengthy trips. No pleas on her part could alleviate the "confinement" which he had imposed upon her. Somehow she managed to look for love and consolation with another man.

It is almost impossible to describe how many factors played a role in the behavior of this woman. Her need for protection and love and her—perhaps unconscious—revenge on her husband are only two of the more important factors. Without justifying her action, we can say that her action was a mixture of self-protection, self-fulfillment and revenge. It seems more a distorted cry for help and attention than a sin. One may even doubt whether it was an act of infidelity toward her husband but rather an attempt to awaken his love and make him pay reasonable attention to her, however unfortunate and distorted that attempt may have been.

Cases like this are not as rare as we like to think. In different matters and in a variety of forms and degrees we see in almost every human action the interaction between unconscious needs and deliberate self-determination. It is always an effort of the individual to come to a self-fulfillment.

But the chosen form of self-fulfillment may be harmful for the realization of one's ultimate self-fulfillment, and then such actions are often called "sins."

As we have indicated earlier, the word "sin" is too easily used to indicate the material action, what is done, instead of the self-expression of the human being. Unsurprisingly, therefore, different sciences can assign a different value to the same human action in certain cases. This is clearly stated by Egenter and Matussek in their book *Moral Problems and Mental Health*: "For the moral theologian adultery is always reprehensible, it is always a sin. For the psychotherapist, however, it may represent something essentially positive in individual cases—a step in the direction of human maturity." [10] It is our belief that even in such cases the psychotherapist doesn't call adultery an advisable and good approach to the solution of the person's problems. But if the person, driven by inner needs, performs such an action, the psychotherapist will not condemn, but rather help the person to use this event toward his or her personal maturity and self-fulfillment. In this context the term "sin" should be used with the utmost care.

In general and abstract terms we may call adultery a sin, namely, insofar as it is—again in general and abstract terms—a serious deviation from the constructive individual and social self-expression which manifests God's law. But sin is real only in the concrete living reality of man's concrete self-expression. Now, in this concrete expression actions that are otherwise undesirable may be positive contributions toward the full growth of personal maturity. Thus they can become a positive step toward man's fuller self-realization in which he must be God's image. The situation may be compared to that of a little child who necessarily falls many times before he is able to walk steadily. Or we may compare it with the incoherent sounds and the wrong use of words by one who is learning to speak. No one will advise a person to utter such incoherent and defective sounds or to perform such actions for their own sake. They are not called good or desirable except insofar as they lead to a more perfect human expression. It follows, therefore, that they should rarely also be called evil. The word "sin" in its traditional meaning should be used with the utmost care. We should rather look at the fulfillment of the human self in its total perspective and then try to see what this particular action does to it.

From the foregoing it should be evident that an accurate distinction between "venial" and "mortal" sin is beyond any human judgment. A mortal sin in the guise of total aversion from God will be an extremely rare phenomenon. Even if man knows that "God's law" as proposed by the Church or by human society demands or forbids a certain action, there is still the inner need and urge of the person that enters into the human self-expression. A total and complete "yes" or "no" can rarely, if ever, be given in human circumstances. Almost all human actions contain some degree of genuine self-fulfillment which includes man's relationship with God. In our earlier example of the woman who committed adultery, one can hardly speak of a total rejection of God and his law. This doesn't mean that we want to minimize the seriousness of her action. There is something dreadfully wrong with her and with her marriage, and something must be done; otherwise she herself and her marriage could suffer greatly. Then a full rejection of God might become a reality. From the viewpoint of self-determination in human self-fulfillment we should perhaps make the same distinction again between venial sin, serious sin and sin unto death. This would help us to see mortal sin not as an individual action, but as a deliberately defective human self-realization in which self-centeredness is the major guiding principle.

3. *Material Values in Human Self-Fulfillment.* Man is by his nature a corporeal-spiritual being. He doesn't exist as an

isolated individual but is essentially related to the human community. Therefore, human self-fulfillment can never reach its fullness except in and through bodily expression and in relation to the human community. This holds for both successful and defective human self-fulfillment. Earlier we have stated that the material perspective alone can never form the ultimate basis for evaluating the morality of a human action. "Matter" in itself has no morality or moral value. It enters the field of morality only to the extent that it becomes the object of the human action or the means of human self-expression. Taking something which is not my own property enters into the moral perspective only to the extent that this action is the expression of my individual self-realization and of my relation to my fellow man.

Human intention alone, however, does not indicate the morality of action either. Man is more than intention. He is also a corporeal and social being. To take or to destroy someone else's property in order to help a person in need may be a very generous and praiseworthy intention, but this does not make the action necessarily good. We have tried to explain earlier how the intention, the goal or the purpose of the action does not justify the action but gives a human meaning to it. Whether or not this human meaning can be "humanly acceptable" must be seen in the context of the human totality to the extent that this is within the reach of human understanding.

However, since the human experience and the interhuman relationship is always somehow connected with material reality, it seems evident that the material perspectives form one of the major elements in the formation of a human judgment. The anger of one person against another is noticeable in time and space in its material expression. In human judgment we must assume that a person who sets fire to his neighbor's house has more anger toward him than the one who throws a stone through the kitchen window. This judgment is not necessarily correct, because the personalities of both "enemies" play an important role in the way anger will be expressed toward one another. But since the bodily aspect of man is the way by which his inner self is expressed in time and space, we may assume that the degree of seriousness of the material effect is in reasonable proportion to the inner reality.

Second, bodily expression is important insofar as it expresses the interhuman or social relationship, and it is a measure of its constructive or destructive influence. To set fire to the neighbor's house has a greater social or interhuman impact than the breaking of a window. It carries heavier responsibility for the person who did it. And the person who performed this act of arson is correctly considered as more dangerous to the human society than the window-smasher.

These two aspects of personal self-realization and interhuman perspective are completely interwoven also in the material or corporeal expression. They are one of the human norms to evaluate the morality of the human action. Although it may never be taken as the ultimate norm for evaluation, it should never be disregarded either. If in the interhuman relationship and in the perspective of the human totality a certain action is harmful or unacceptable, then there is something wrong with the action. In an individual case there may be no personal sinfulness involved, but that does not make an action unqualifiedly good. Its *material* evil effect falls under the responsibility of the agent and he will be responsible to repair the damage as well as he can.

Let us go back to the example of the woman who committed adultery. Let us assume that on a *strictly personal* level there was no serious sin involved and that it was, on the contrary, a positive step toward greater personal maturity and better marital relationship. Yet she carries a child which is not her husband's. There is an extra financial burden and a circumstance which may develop into a continuous source of mutual distrust, not to mention other possibly unfortunate consequences. For these consequences she carries at least part of the responsibility, and it will be her task of human self-realization to restrict these unfortunate consequences as well as she can.

This gives us a rather correct insight into what moral theologians have traditionally called "material" or "objective" sin. This term denotes that on the perceptible plane there are failures in human self-fulfillment. These perceptible failures constitute the external ground for an evaluation of the human action, without being the ultimate norm for their moral value. These same perceptible failures delineate the responsibility of the agent to "make restitution" for the harm which he has caused. The obligation to make restitution, then, should not be reduced to a merely penal law, which is to be fulfilled only under force of external legislation. On the contrary, it is part of the human self-realization and self-fulfillment. Man is personally responsible for his actions and their consequences, even if his actions come partially forth from his inner unconscious needs and urges.

Human self-fulfillment is a continuous dynamic expression of life with unavoidable successes and failures. Both success and failure should not be considered in the perspective of the individual action only, but in the perspective of the human totality. Moral evaluation can never adequately be expressed in terms of the material reality, but only the human totality can be the norm. The law of God is not written in material structures, but in the human reality as a whole. This human reality as a whole is man created to the image of God, while the depth-dimension of his existence is revealed in Christ. Human and Christian perfection, therefore, is not situated in the performance of good actions and in the avoidance of sin. Human and Christian perfection is to become the living expression of God's presence in humanity. This self-becoming of man is a slow process of growth in which he must feel his way. Formulated laws, structures and organization are indispensable aids, but ultimately it is man himself who through stumbling and failing must give his human response to God's invitation.

NOTES

1. James Gustafson, *Christ and the Moral Life* (Harper and Row, New York, 1968), p. 106.
2. Marc Oraison, *Morality for Our Time* (Doubleday, New York, 1968), pp. 107–108.
3. John McKenzie, *Dictionary of the Bible* (Bruce, Milwaukee, 1965), pp. 817–819.
4. C. Spicq, *Theologie Morale de Nouveau Testament* (Desclée, Paris, Vol. I), p. 196.
5. McKenzie, *op. cit.*, p. 820.
6. Jean Giblet, *A Commentary on St. Paul's Epistle to the Romans* (American College, Louvain, 1968), p. 54.
7. Jean Giblet, *op. cit.*, p. 164.
8. Jean Giblet, *op. cit.*, p. 175.
9. William van der Marck, "Het onvoorziene Risico van Augustinus' Erfzondeleer voor de Huwelijkstheologie," in *Tijdschrift voor Theologie* (1967), pp. 31–33.
10. R. Egenter/P. Matussek, *Moral Problems and Mental Health* (Alba House, 1970), p. 60.